wild food

for free

wild food

for free

Jonathan Hilton

First published in Great Britain in 2007
by Hamlyn, a division of
Octopus Publishing Group Ltd
2–4 Heron Quays, London E14 4JP

Copyright © Octopus Publishing
Group Ltd 2007
Text copyright © Jonathan Hilton 2007

ISBN-13: 978-1-85675-285-5
ISBN-10: 1-85675-285-2

A CIP catalogue record for this book is
available from the British Library

Printed and bound in China

10 9 8 7 6 5 4 3 2 1

Publisher's Notes

Information contained in this book is
for information purposes only and neither
the author nor the publisher accepts any
liability for any injury or death occurring
as a result of ingesting or exposure to any
wild foods described in the book. Foraging
for wild food is entirely at the reader's own
risk and the use of the information in this
book implies the reader's acknowledgement
and acceptance of these facts.

Both metric and imperial measurements are
given for the recipes. Use one set of measures
only, not a mixture of both.

This books includes dishes made with nuts and
nut derivatives. It is advisable for those with
known allergic reactions to nuts and nut
derivatives and those who may be potentially
vulnerable to these allergies, such as pregnant
and nursing mothers, invalids, the elderly,
babies and children, to avoid dishes made with
nuts and nut oils.

Meat and poultry should be cooked thoroughly.
To test if poultry is cooked, pierce the flesh
through the thickest part with a skewer or fork –
the juices should run clear, never pink or red.

Warning

Many wild foods are poisonous, even
fatally poisonous. Foragers should
always identify by all indicators
before eating from the wild. Different
plants might look very similar to the
untrained eye. If you do collect wild
foods to eat make sure that all of the
identification checks for each species
are carried out in detail to avoid
poisonous look-alikes. IF IN ANY
DOUBT DO NOT EAT THE WILD
FOOD. Beginners should never eat
wild foods until they have had their
own identifications checked by an
expert in the field.

Certain species of wild fungi can
cause an allergic reaction in people
with no prior food allergies.
Therefore when eating a wild fungus
for the first time it is important that
you eat only a very small amount and
wait 24 hours to check for any
allergies or adverse reactions before
eating more. If you do have an
adverse reaction, seek medical
attention immediately. It will greatly
assist with any treatment if you are
able to bring a sample or identify
what caused the reaction.

The author and publisher have made
every effort to ensure accuracy in this
book, but the responsibility for eating
any wild foods must rest with the
individual. You are ultimately
responsible for your own education,
actions and diet. Neither the
publisher nor the author accept
responsibility for any effects that may
arise from eating any wild food.

Contents

INTRODUCTION

Learning just a little about the types of plants that not only are safe to eat but also taste good has nothing to do with survival, for unless some unforeseen disaster occurs, survival is pretty well guaranteed. It is more a matter of learning to reconnect with nature, of feeling comfortable and at ease in the countryside, no matter where you happen to be.

Foraging for wild food

If only we knew it, we are literally surrounded by good, wholesome, wild food. Nature's own vegetable market is laid out before us, containing virtually everything we need for a sustainable, balanced diet and a healthy life – and it's all for free.

The amount of the planet's surface currently under cultivation is extensive and ever-increasing as world population rises annually. But more and more of this cultivated land is being turned over to fewer and fewer crops. Millions of hectares of agricultural land are not only devoted to growing the same species of food plants, but very often those endless fields are growing precisely the same genetically enhanced, high-yield, fertilizer-dependent variety. As a result, high-performance crops are making us vulnerable to a range of natural calamities; at present a full one-third of all food crops grown worldwide are destroyed by either insect attacks or plant diseases before they can even be harvested.

An ever-closer focus

We have not always been reliant on just a few food crops. You may be surprised to discover that throughout recorded history more than 10,000 species of food plants (including fungi and seaweeds) are known to have been used by different cultures. It is realistic to assume that the same number again of potentially edible plants are out there somewhere, unsampled. Of the 10,000 known species of food plants, only about 150

have ever been cultivated to any significant extent. It is from this genetic pool that nearly all of today's commercial food plants are derived, having been selectively bred to produce more seed per plant, sturdier stems, bigger leaves, larger flowerheads, earlier cropping, heavier crops or whatever it is that we decide is most desirable.

This process of ever-closer focus on fewer food plants means that today, fully 90 per cent of the world's food requirements are provided by just 20 species of plant, and out of these 20 species, just three species of grass – maize, wheat and rice – satisfy more than 50 per cent of the world's calorie requirements.

Remaking old connections

It's not too late to reconnect with nature's wild larder. I doubt there is a single person who has not gone blackberry or raspberry picking and been captivated by the succulent sweetness of these fully ripe berries plucked directly from the bush. Or perhaps as a child you knew of an old walnut tree or wild plum in some abandoned,

Nature offers us good, wholesome wild food such as the delicious fruits of this wild cherry tree.

long-derelict garden or hedgerow. Or was there a wild strawberry patch just off your path to school, and can you deny that the flavour of those small, irregular fruits was better than anything you have ever tasted from the shelves of a supermarket?

Well, that old walnut tree might be gone, the hedgerow succumbed to housing development and that strawberry patch uprooted, but these and hundreds of other edible species of plants, fungi and seaweeds are still there for you to rediscover and enjoy. The blackberries might still be going strong, being tenacious beasts once they take hold.

A word about safety
The knowledge that some plants are edible and some are not has often been hard won, coming down to us from a time when the only way to know whether a plant was safe was a matter of trial and error, and then to note the reactions. In some instances, those reactions were serious and sometimes fatal – many of the most lethal poisons were originally derived from the plant world, although they are now more likely to be synthesized.

More often, however, plants were simply unpalatable rather than lethal, although many could well lead to short-term digestive disorders and some to hallucinations. In the same way, many plants were discovered to be of medicinal value rather than being useful as food, and as high-tech as our modern medicine is today, the overwhelming proportion of the drugs we rely on are either derived directly from or are synthetics inspired by substances discovered in the plant kingdom.

Trial and error will definitely not do anymore. You will find this principle stated many times throughout this book, but it cannot be stressed too often – if you do not know for certain that a plant is safe to eat, leave it alone.

Using this book
The following chapters are divided into broadly defined habitats – places where plants prefer to grow. This approach allows you to thoroughly explore a particular area for its edible potential.

If you are not intending to go out looking for very specific plants, but know, for example, that you will be holidaying by the coast, camping in a wooded area or will be staying somewhere surrounded by grass and prairie land, this chapter arrangement allows you to read up on some of

Though not as large as its cultivated counterpart, the fruit of the wild strawberry is sweet and succulent.

Tenacious and able to colonize neglected land, the blackberry has been part of our diet for thousands of years.

the plants you are most likely to encounter to allow you to enjoy finding them.

If, however, you intend to look for specific herbs, fruits, nuts, seeds and so on, then you can pull out the relevant information from the different chapters and decide the most sensible time of the year to start foraging. If the peak time for a particular flower is late summer to early autumn, you will have a guide to when it is best to start looking for it. Likewise, you will know in advance that if the best-tasting shoots of some other plants are available in early spring, you should start looking then.

These times, as well as information relating to eventual height and spread of plants, can only ever be regarded as approximate. So much depends on microclimates, how far north or south you are situated, and the specifics of the seasons in any particular year. In light of this, you should use your knowledge of local conditions to decide when to go foraging. After a typical winter, early spring might well be March, but a particularly harsh winter might push the onset of spring forward to mid-April. However, an especially mild winter might mean early spring commences around mid-February.

The final chapter of the book is the one that makes all your efforts worthwhile. You will find a range of delicious recipes using all the wild foods found in the book. Happy foraging!

The do's and don'ts of plant collecting

Even though food collecting from the wild is, for most foragers, a harmless and enjoyable weekend pastime, there are still some rules you need to be aware of.

Not only is foraging a thoroughly enjoyable and inexpensive way of putting excellent wild food on the table, it is also an ideal way to experience a whole range of new flavours. These novel and often more subtle and surprising tastes will be quite different from the taste of cultivated vegetables you are used to eating from your local greengrocer, market stall or supermarket. And the pleasure derived from being out in the woods, walking the hills, beachcombing at low tide, and using your knowledge and experience to gather a totally natural product, is beyond value. What a wonderful way to connect with nature and with the lives of our ancestors, thinking perhaps of what it must have been like when knowing how and where to find wild food really did matter.

However, the nature of wild food is that its continuing existence is precarious, relying as it does on the right conditions – habitat, rainfall, sunshine, temperatures and so on – without any benevolent interference from outside sources. This puts a tremendous responsibility on all of us to do the right thing, to remain sensitive to the needs of the plants we are harvesting, as well as the environment we find them in, so that they will be there the next year and the year after that for others to enjoy after us.

Legal concerns

You do not have the right to enter on to private land in order to collect plant material. If relevant, always obtain permission from the landowner and make sure that they know you want to collect plants and there is no objection. The margins of a cultivated field, for example, may be too awkward for ploughing and

Traditional pursuits

Picking wild nuts, fruit, leaves, berries and fungi (see pages 18–19) is a traditional countryside activity stretching back countless generations. It probably does no harm as long as the plants are growing abundantly in the locality and you take only what you need for your immediate use. Try not to take extra produce for freezing or drying in order to avoid depleting your food supply. Always ensure you leave enough seed behind to grow into the next generation and keep safe practice uppermost in your mind – never, for example, use any plant or part of a plant picked from the wild that you have not positively identified as being safe to eat.

planting, but that does not mean that any uncultivated plants growing there are up for grabs. If the landowner does give permission, then take the opportunity to find out what, if any, fertilizers, herbicides or pesticides have been used on the land (see also pages 16–17), as these factors directly affect the edibility of any plants you may find.

Even plants that are growing wild in the countryside are the legal property of somebody, of some authority or organization, and it is almost certainly illegal to harvest them on anything even vaguely resembling a commercial scale or if you are plant collecting with a view to making money from your endeavours. It is very unlikely, however, that collecting from a few plants for your personal use is going to do any damage or attract attention. Uprooting plants, however, is different (see below).

Uprooting plants for commercial purposes or personal use, even those growing on public land, without express permission is not only irresponsible, but it is almost certainly illegal, though this may vary from region to region and country to country. Many of the descriptions of plants in the following chapters state that the roots, bulbs, rhizomes and so on are edible and can be used for cooking, but even where it is permitted to dig up a plant to get at these parts, you should do so only if the plant is growing well in that area and it is abundant. You should also take great care to ensure that your efforts do not unnecessarily disturb or compact the surrounding soil or damage nearby plants.

If you see a group of mushrooms growing in an empty field, you don't necessarily have the legal right to pick them.

Good practice

There are some practical things you can do to ensure you make the best use of your time, finding and collecting as much good-quality produce as you need in the shortest possible time.

- Pick only from healthy-looking plants. Ignore leaves that are showing signs of damage or wilt, shoots that are limp or have poor colour or fruit, berries and nuts that appear to have been attacked by insects, birds or other wildlife. (And take care when picking soft fruit and berries that you don't inadvertently damage them through rough handling and so reduce their shelf life.) With many species of fungi, you need to look out for insect infestation, especially with older specimens that may have gone a little spongy.

Cow parsley requires careful identification in the wild because of its similarity to deadly hemlock.

- Foraging on a warm, sunny day simply makes a good walk even better, and the best time to go out is a few days after a good downpour of rain. Plants are often invigorated after a thorough soaking, putting out a burst of energy in the form of succulent new growth. In addition, the rain also cleans the foliage of any surface pollution. Wait a few days after the rain, to give the soil a chance to absorb all the moisture and allow it to cope better with any foot traffic without becoming compacted.

- If you are collecting bark, take it from the smallest suitable branches or twigs. Do not remove bark from large branches or the main stem or trunk. If you need to remove a complete branch, use a sharp blade or pruning saw and cut it cleanly in order to minimize the chance of disease entering the wound. Take care when using a blade or saw that you do not accidentally damage adjacent branches.

- Do not be tempted to introduce useful edible plants into your wild locality that do not naturally grow there just to make foraging easier for yourself. You simply cannot predict how the local balance of nature will be disturbed by any new introductions.

When to pick

The best time of day or season to collect from plants in the wild depends on a number of factors:

- For some plants, as well as most fungi, it is best to make an early start and fill your collecting basket before the sun has dried the dew from the ground.

- For herbs, which are intended to impart their unique flavour to other foods, it is better to pick during the hottest part of the afternoon. This is when the flowers of many herb plants tend to be at their best for picking.

- If collecting seed, the general guideline is to wait approximately a month after flowering has finished before gathering seed. If, for example, the flowering period is between June and August, you could start looking for ripe seed some time after September. There will always be exceptions, of course, and there is no substitute for experience.

- Collecting roots and bulbs could involve digging deep into the ground, a task made easier when the soil is thoroughly moist in spring and autumn. Be careful where you walk, however, in order to minimize damage to the surrounding soil. Rhizomes are often suggested for collecting, but since these usually grow at the surface or just beneath, they are not so much of a problem.

- Fruits, nuts and berries are the staple for most foragers and must usually be collected when they are ripe or just before for a slightly longer shelf life. In most instances, autumn is the time of year for this, but use your local knowledge to judge which part of the season is likely to be best. Pick too soon and they will be lacking flavour; wait too long and they may be overripe.

General safety tips

In these times of mass urbanization, many people live in towns and cities, where they are effectively cut off from the centres of food production in the surrounding countryside. For this reason some general advice on safe foraging is required.

In this modern world we live in, it's not surprising that most of us have lost touch with the wild food growing all around and so simply don't know what is good and safe to eat any more and what is not.

The best way to learn the ropes is to go out searching for wild food in the company of an experienced forager, somebody who can point out the salient features of different local plants so that you then recognize the ones suitable for the kitchen at the various stages of their growing cycles. It is even more important to learn about the unpleasant-tasting or dangerous plants so that you can steer well clear of them to avoid any potential health problems.

Since even old hands at this eating-for-free business can make mistakes, if you are not absolutely certain of your identification, or if any environmental factors are a concern to you, then follow these general guidelines.

Environmental factors
- If plants are growing on waste ground near houses or other buildings, or in parks and managed woodland, they may have been contaminated with pesticides. The same is true of plants growing on the margins or the general vicinity of cultivated farmland. Wash all plants gathered in these situations especially carefully before eating them.

- Plants growing on roadside verges are likely to have picked up a coating of pollutants from the exhausts of passing vehicles. Since most fuel on sale now is lead-free, this is a tremendous help in lessening the pollution load, but nevertheless wash plants growing close to roads with particular care before eating them.

- Plants growing in or near stagnant water could be contaminated with a range of parasites able to cause gastric distress or worse. Don't eat such plants raw in salads, but boil them first for at least a few minutes to kill off any bugs. Likewise, plants growing in or near drainage ditches removing the run-off from farmland could be contaminated with both inorganic fertilizers and pesticides.

Play it safe
- As a general rule, it is not wise to eat any fruit that is over ripe and starting to spoil or is badly bruised. Even fruit that is normally perfectly safe to eat can become toxic to some degree in these circumstances.

- Most people know that cyanide smells of almonds, so avoid eating any part of a plant that has that familiar almond scent. The almond itself belongs to the *Prunus* species, along with the cherry and wild plum. The fruits of these trees are almost certainly safe to eat, but if you encounter a fruit or nut that is particularly bitter or has an intense almond-like aroma, do not eat it.

- Bear in mind that you may have a particular sensitivity to a plant that is normally perfectly safe to eat, so if you have never tasted it before, hold it in contact with the outside of your lips for a few minutes. If there is no reaction, place a small portion on your tongue for another few minutes; again, if there is no reaction, thoroughly chew a tiny portion. If once more you do not react in a couple of minutes, then it is probably safe for you to eat.

- In general, avoid plants that have a milky coloured sap and don't eat beans or seed pods, apart from those on plants you know to be safe.

Caution

There is no room for error when it comes to eating fungi – either you know for certain what species you are dealing with and that it is safe to eat or you leave it strictly alone (see pages 18–19 for further information). With some species of fungi, it can be many hours after ingesting a portion that symptoms occur for the first time.

There can be danger even in familiar foods, such as the almond, as explained on pages 44–45.

Safety with fungi

You cannot be too safety conscious when it comes to foraging for fungi, as eating some species can cause illness or even death. However, if you follow these guidelines, it shouldn't be too long before you are collecting with cautious confidence.

An early start with the promise of a sunny day to come, this is the best time of day to go foraging for fungi – or 'mushrooming' as it is sometimes called.

However, you need to bear firmly in mind that making a mistake can have serious, sometimes fatal, consequences. There are lots of safety rules concerning fungi, but the Golden Rule, the rule that must never be broken is 'if in doubt, leave it out'. Do not rely on any of the traditional 'shortcuts' to safety when it comes to distinguishing edible and poisonous species,

The poisonous panther cap shown here is very similar in appearance to the harmless grey-spotted amanita.

such as brightly coloured ones are poisonous or caps that are easy to peel are safe. Some of these statements may be true for some species, but none is true for all.

Staying safe
- Go fungus hunting with an expert. Check to see if there is a local society or club and take advantage of any available expertise.
- Use the best possible field notes and identification photographs or artworks, but bear in mind that the size, shape and colour of fungi of the same species are extremely variable.
- Do not collect immature specimens since they usually do not display all the features necessary for a positive identification.
- If a specimen differs in even one respect from the characteristics noted for that species, play safe and do not pick it.
- Be aware of the precise features that distinguish your 'edible' fungi from any potentially toxic 'look-alike' species.
- Don't assume your knowledge is transferable to different countries – for example, in Europe, a particular species may have no poisonous look-alikes, while in North or South America, that may not be the case.

Preparing fungi

Never carry or store fungi in sealed plastic bags or plastic boxes, as the lack of air and humid conditions hasten decay, turning a mouth-watering feast into something rather unpleasant and probably smelly. Leave them in a wicker basket, allowing air to circulate; drape an absorbent paper towel over the top to keep the sun off and deter flies. Fungi, especially older specimens, are prone to insect infestation, especially maggots. Inspect your finds closely and cut off and discard any maggoty, soggy or musty-smelling areas.

Before cooking, use a soft brush or a damp cloth to clean off any soil, leaf litter, twigs and other debris. Remove at least the end of the stem that is hard and heavily soiled, and with some species you need to discard the whole of the stem. With a few exceptions you should never wash fungi. Usually, it is not necessary to peel fungi unless the skin is damaged, soiled or slimy. As you slice the cap for cooking, keep a close eye out for any insects that you may disturb. Unless you intend to freeze or dry your finds, always prepare and cook them as soon as possible as they generally do not keep well.

- If you discover that you have collected a poisonous fungus and mixed it in with your edible species, play safe and dispose of them all in case of contamination.
- When trying a new species of fungus, keep a small portion of it uncooked in the refrigerator to aid in identification in case you have a bad reaction.

Both the death cap (above top) and the destroying angel (above bottom) are fatally poisonous.

Identifying plants

The forager's enjoyment of collecting and eating wild foods can be greatly enhanced by a basic understanding of a few specialized terms. Use this guide to help you describe and identify the wonderful edible plants nature has to offer.

Introduction

Those with an interest in finding and describing plants soon fall into the habit of using at least some specialized terms – a working jargon – in order to communicate as accurately and succinctly as possible with others. If we all speak the same language, then this type of technical shorthand is both quick and efficient; if we don't, then it is simply confusing. The following photographs of flowers, leaves, roots and fungi will help to explain some of the less-familiar terms used in this book.

The accurate identification of wild plants, such as this hawthorn, is essential to the success of your foraging.

FLOWERS

Cup-shaped petals

Bell-shaped petals

Tubular petals

Cross-shaped petals

Star-shaped petals

Reflexed petals

Spike flowers

Cyme flowers

Umbel flowers

Raceme flowers

Panicle flowers

Cluster flowers

LEAVES

Terminal flowers

Axillary flowers

Toothed (serrated)

Entire

Wavy (undulate)

Scalloped

Lobed divisions

Palmate divisions

Pinnate divisions

Opposite arrangement

Alternate arrangement

Simple arrangement

Basal rosette arrangement

Oblong

Elliptic

Lance-shaped

Cordate (heart-shaped)

Ovate

ROOTS

Obovate

Spear-shaped

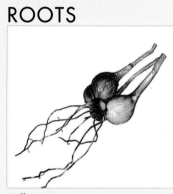

Bulb

Rhizome

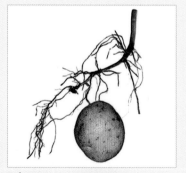

Tuber

Taproot

FUNGI

Convex cap

Concave cap

Flat cap

Bell-shaped cap

Conical cap

In-rolled cap

Wavy cap

Central cap attachment

Excentric cap attachment

WOODLAND PLANTS

The forest and woods are the repositories for much of the planet's biodiversity; our green inheritance. Out there among the trees is nature's larder, a treasure house overflowing with fruits and seeds, leaves and berries, nuts and roots – food not just to sustain the body, but also to delight the senses. And so much of this potential bonanza lies wasted and uncollected, often passed-by simply because we've forgotten that good food can be free.

Allium ursinum

Wild garlic

broad, lance-shaped leaves • forms large carpeting clumps • garlic aroma to leaves • excellent flavouring for salads, sauces and stews

Woodland Plants

What is it?
A bulbous, perennial plant. Grows up to 45 cm (18 in) high.

What to look for
Wild garlic grows in fens and also in damp woodlands. The deep-green leaves are broad and lance-like. Colonies can be invasive and a distinctive garlic odour apparent. It comes into growth in mid- to late winter, flowers in spring through to early summer (April to June) and dies back by mid-summer. The white, star-like flowers are held in umbels well clear of the leaves.

Can be mistaken for
Lily of the valley (*Convallaria majalis*) and autumn crocus (*Colchicum autumnale*), although both of these plants bear only the slightest resemblance to wild garlic and neither has the merest trace of a garlic odour.

Where to look
Wild garlic prefers semi-shade, under trees and moist soil conditions. It tolerates quite wet soil conditions in winter. It is often found in fenlands and around drainage ditches associated with hedgerows. This is a Europe-wide plant.

When to look for it
The leaves can be used in mid- to late January where winters are relatively mild. In mid-spring you can start to harvest the flowers and continue right through while the seeds ripen. The bulb can be eaten throughout the year.

What does it taste like?
The leaves have a pleasant, surprisingly mild flavour of garlic. The flavour of the flowers

The star-like flowers of wild garlic are hermaphrodite, containing both male and female reproductive organs.

intensifies as the seeds ripen. The bulb has the strongest flavour, though still milder than cultivated garlic bulbs (*Allium sativum*).

How is it used?
The leaves can be eaten raw or cooked. Raw leaves make a perfect addition to a winter salad, while the cooked leaves add a subtle flavour to sauces, soups and stews. Try using it as a flavour enhancer for otherwise bland foods, such as cottage cheese. The bulbs, which are full of flavour, are small and can be eaten raw or cooked.

Try it in
Wild Garlic Pasta (see page 206).

Caution
There have been reports of toxicity among dogs when wild garlic is eaten in large quantities.

Forager's checklist

- ✔ Broad, lance-like, dark-green leaves
- ✔ White, star-like flowers
- ✔ Flowers borne on stalks well above the leaves
- ✔ Distinctive aroma of garlic to leaves and flowers
- ✔ Member of the onion family, leaves also reminiscent of the smell of chives

Wild Garlic

The strap- or lance-like leaves and umbels of white flowers make wild garlic a distinctive-looking plant.

Castanea sativa

Sweet chestnut

handsome tree • oblong to elliptical leaves • spikes of prominent flowers • nuts can be roasted and eaten or ground to make flour

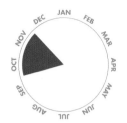

Woodland Plants

What is it?
A tall deciduous tree. Grows up to 35 m (115 ft) high although 18 m (60 ft) is more usual, with a spread of about half its height.

Each spiny, prickly burr of the sweet chestnut contains between one and five delicious nuts.

What to look for
Sweet chestnut leaves are glossy green, oblong to elliptical with prominent, parallel veining and coarsely serrated margins. The bark of older trees is deeply fissured and often spirally ridged. The summer flowers are creamy yellow, strongly scented and grow in catkins. Glossy brown nuts develop within a prickly burr. There can be up to five nuts in a single burr, but those cultivars that produce a single, large, sweet nut are highly prized.

Can be mistaken for
The sweet chestnut tree is not related to the horse chestnut (*Aesculus*), with its inedible nuts.

Forager's checklist

✔ Strongly scented flower catkins in summer

✔ Dark-green, serrated-edged leaves

✔ Leaves take on autumn colour before nuts ripen

✔ When ripe, the nut starts to split the prickly outer husk

Where to look

An open woodland tree, which can also be found on the fringes of meadows. Commonly found in parks. It can grow successfully on poor soil, and tolerates drought conditions well once established, though it must have full sun. This is a Europe-wide plant.

When to look for it

The nuts require the warmth of a long summer to ripen properly, so harvest this tree's bounty around October or November.

What does it taste like?

Once stripped of their outer casing and inner pith, the nuts lose much of their bitterness and can be eaten raw. Once roasted in the oven, however, or in the embers of an open fire, the fleshy inner nut becomes sweet and succulent.

How is it used?

Chestnuts have higher starch and lower oil contents than many other nuts. Slit the shells before roasting to prevent the nut exploding. Flavour the flesh with butter and a little freshly ground black pepper. In southern Europe, chestnuts are ground to make a gluten-free flour. In Italy, chestnut flour was the basis of polenta before the introduction of corn. The flesh can also be boiled and mashed to make a potato substitute.

Try it in

Chocolate Chestnut Truffles (see page 207).

Sweet Chestnut

The sweet chestnut tree produces its largest, sweetest nuts after enjoying a warm, dry summer.

Corylus avellana

Hazel

forms a dense thicket • large shrub or small tree • nuts ripen in
autumn • male catkins develop in winter • small female flowers
appear in spring

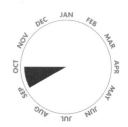

What is it?
A dense thicket of straight, upright stems forming
a large deciduous shrub or small tree. Height
and width between 3.5 and 8 m (12 and 25 ft).

What to look for
The 5–10 cm (2–4 in) leaves are toothed,
alternate and slightly hairy, more so on the under
surface. The yellowy-brown catkins are the male
flowers, which appear on bare branches in
February. Look carefully for the inconspicuous
red female flowers, which bloom in early spring.
The hazelnuts develop in clusters of 2–4.

Where to look
This plant often grows as an under-storey in oak
woodlands or can be found as part of hedges.
Hazel grows best in dappled shade. It does not
tolerate acid soils and is widely distributed
throughout Europe.

When to look for it
Do not collect hazelnuts too early, as the flesh
will be soft and lacking in flavour. Leave it too
late, however, and you will be competing with
squirrels and birds. Wait until the leaves take on
their yellow autumn colour between September
and October.

The nuts of the hazel develop in small
clusters and are ready for picking in
autumn once the leaves start to turn.

Forager's checklist

✔ Evidence of small red flowers in summer

✔ Simple, alternate, toothed leaves

✔ If the shell turns dark brown, the nut has probably disintegrated

✔ Wait for the leaves to turn yellow in autumn before harvesting

What does it taste like?

The hazel is an excellent nut to eat raw. The oval-shaped kernel has an agreeable, mild, starchy flavour and is distinctly oily – not surprising since the hazelnut contains, weight for weight, seven times more fat than hens' eggs.

How is it used?

The nut can be eaten raw or roasted to enhance its flavour. If kept in their shells (in a dark, dry place), hazelnuts should store successfully for up to a year. In their raw or roasted state, hazel nuts are used to add flavour and texture to cakes, breads and biscuits. Being rich in oil, they can also be processed in a liquidizer and used as a milk substitute. The yellow-tinged oil from hazelnuts can be used in salad dressings and as an intense flavour enhancer in baking.

The flowers of the hazel are either male or female, but it is self-fertile as both sexes are found growing on the same plant.

Crataegus monogyna

Hawthorn

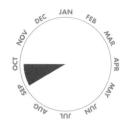

long, sharp thorns on slender stems • serrated tips to leaf lobes •
small white or pinkish flowers • widely distributed • leaves and
fruit can be harvested

Woodland Plants

What is it?
A large deciduous shrub or small tree. Can
grow 6–9 m (20–30 ft) high and produces a
broad, rounded head. If left unpruned it may
reach 15 m (50 ft) or so.

What to look for
Simple, lobed, dark-green leaves have toothed
(serrated) tips and grow in an alternate
arrangement from slightly pendulous branches.
Its long thorns are a distinctive feature. Masses
of small white or pink flowers are borne in
corymbs in May. These make a showy display
but are short-lived – up to about ten days only,
depending on the weather.

Where to look
Hawthorn can grow in heavy clay soil and in
ground that is nutritionally poor, but does not
like wet peat. It is often the most common
component in hedges, where it copes well with
both neglect and constant pruning. Apart from
being found in hedges, hawthorn is a common
woodland and scrubland plant. It tolerates
shade but prefers full sun. It is drought-hardy
once established and is widely distributed
throughout Europe.

When to look for it
The hawthorn flowers in late spring to early
summer – around May and June. The flowers
carry both male and female organs and
pollination is often by midges. The fruit ripens
from September through to October, when the
plant can be laden with bunches of red berries
(hawes). These are very attractive to wildlife.

The fruit of the hawthorn contains up
to five individual seeds, but these
tend to stick together.

What does it taste like?

The uncooked fruit or hawes of the hawthorn do not have a particularly notable flavour and have been described as having 'a fresh, fruity, mealy taste'.

How is it used?

The fruit is used in making preserves and jams, and can be added to the medley of ingredients in 'hedgerow jam'. The dried fruit can be ground and added to flour used for baking. Young shoots can be used raw as a salad ingredient. The leaves make an acceptable tea substitute. In fact, at times when tea was a rare commodity, hawthorn leaves were sometimes added to bulk out available supplies. Finally, hawthorn flowers can be added to a fresh fruit salad or used to flavour syrups and puddings. They also work well when added to custards and junkets.

Forager's checklist

- ✔ Mature bark flakes off in irregular scales
- ✔ Masses of strongly scented flowers in late spring
- ✔ Dark, glossy-green leaves about 7 cm (3 in) long
- ✔ Tolerates atmospheric pollution
- ✔ Fast-growing

Hawthorn

Modern research bears out the old folk belief that the flowers of the hawthorn are beneficial for the heart.

Fagus sylvatica

Beech

short-stalked, alternate, simple leaves • buds covered in brown scales • silver-grey wood • impressive domed crown of foliage • flowers appear in late spring

What is it?
The stately 'Queen of the forest' is a deciduous tree that can reach 40 m (130 ft), though half this height is more usual.

What to look for
The leaf cover of the beech is very dense, thus preventing light from reaching the surrounding ground. As a result, the under-storey is often clear of most other forms of plant life. The wavy-edged leaves are simple and alternate, silver coloured and downy when newly emerged, turning smooth and glossy as they age. The dead leaves remain on the tree throughout winter, being displaced by the emerging spring growth. Golden-yellow tassels of male flowers appear around the months of April and May, as do the shorter, stouter, upright stalks of pink and green female flowers.

Where to look
A woodland tree found throughout Europe. Where established, it is often the dominant tree species. Beech trees prefer chalky soils and will tolerate shade to full sun. You can also find beech growing on loamy or sandy soil, as long as it is well drained.

When to look for it
Two triangular-shaped beechnuts, collectively known as 'mast', develop in each four-lobed, prickly husk and are ready for harvesting around October. Heavy nut production occurs only every 5–8 years.

A lubricating oil can be extracted from the seeds, which can be used for polishing and nourishing wood.

Forager's checklist

✔ Leaves are 5–10 cm (2–4 in) long with 5–9 well-marked parallel pairs of veins

✔ Attractive, grey bark

✔ Tree shape is very wide

✔ Male and female flowers on the same tree

What does it taste like?

Young beech leaves have a pleasant, mild flavour. Beechnuts have a distinctly sweet flavour, but they are small and de-husking them is a time-consuming task.

How is it used?

Young beech leaves can be used as a raw ingredient in salads. Use only the youngest leaves, however, as they quickly become tough and unpleasant. Beechnuts can be snacked on raw, though raw nuts are most often used as animal feed, especially for pigs (do not give to horses). Usually, the nuts are dried and ground down before being added to flour. Beechnut oil has been compared favourably with olive oil in taste and makes a flavoursome base for a salad dressing. In some parts of Europe, beechnuts are also roasted, ground and used as a coffee substitute.

Caution

Beechnuts can be toxic if eaten in large quantities.

If picked young enough, the raw leaves of the beech tree make a tasty addition to the salad bowl.

Juglans regia

Walnut

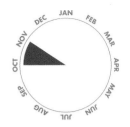

compound, alternate leaves • bright green nut turning brown •
light ash-grey coloured bark • nuts can be pickled, cooked or
eaten raw

Woodland Plants

What is it?
A deciduous tree, generally about 18 m (60 ft)
tall, with a spread to match, but occasionally
reaching heights of 30 m (100 ft).

What to look for
The walnut has a large, distinctive compound
leaf, which can measure 45 cm (18 in) in
length, with 5–7 (sometimes 9) leaflets. Young
leaves are reddish-brown; mature leaves shiny
dark green. The flowers and leaves break at the
same time – late in the season in late spring or
early summer, thereby avoiding the last of the
frosts, to which the new growth is sensitive. The
fat, reddish male catkins are about 5–7 cm

The ripe nuts are delicious eaten raw,
and unripe fruits can be pickled and
preserved in vinegar.

(2–3 in) long, turning more yellowish before
dying. The yellow-green female flowers are
insignificant, growing in small clusters on
the new twigs. The plant is self-fertile and
wind-pollinated.

Can be mistaken for
Juglans regia can be mistaken for the hickory
(*Carya*). To distinguish them, split a twig and
examine the pith – the walnut has distinct air
pockets, while the hickory is solid.

Where to look
More commonly found in the warm-to-hot
regions of southern Europe, the walnut tree
was introduced into more northern regions of
Europe. It must have a position in full sun to
bring its crop of nuts to maturity. It is more likely
to be found in woodland parks rather than
natural woodlands.

When to look for it
The nuts should be ready for harvesting in late
autumn, about October or November. They
should be dried out naturally and be ready for
eating. Nuts can be harvested when they are
still green and wet, around July. If so, they
should be pickled rather than eaten raw.

Walnut

What does it taste like?
A delicious, intense and richly flavoured nut, popular as both a cooking ingredient and also a snack food.

Forager's checklist

✔ Leaves have a sweet, aromatic smell when rubbed between your fingers

✔ Leaf sap stains your fingers

✔ Deeply fissured bark grows in a roughly diamond-shaped pattern

✔ Large, compound leaves with 5–9 leaflets

✔ Surrounding ground often littered with dropped twigs, leaves, branches and nuts

Once thoroughly dried, the young leaves of the walnut tree can be crumbled to make a refreshing tea.

How is it used?
The walnut tree is very versatile. The sap can be tapped in spring and processed to make a sugar substance. Its young leaves can be dried and made into a tea. The nut itself can be picked green and pickled or, when ripe later in the year, eaten raw, roasted, roughly broken into pieces for adding to cake and pudding mixes, or finely ground and added to a wide range of both sweet and savoury dishes. The nut can be pressed to produce a delicious oil for salad dressings or food flavouring. The oil, however, does not store well and quickly deteriorates.

Try it in
Walnut and Two-cheese Pasta (see page 208).

Juniperus communis

Juniper

evergreen, needle-like leaves • both male and female plants must be grown if seed is required • red to grey-brown coloured bark • berries commonly used as a food flavouring

What is it?
Very variable in form, juniper can take the shape of a multi-stemmed, upright evergreen shrub, a prostrate, mat-forming shrub, or a small tree. As a tree it usually grows no more than 5 m (16 ft) high, though occasionally reaches heights of 15 m (50 ft).

What to look for
The evergreen sword-like needles (leaves) of the Juniper are sharply pointed, about 1 cm (½ in) long and grow in whorls of three. The bark of mature plants readily shreds and is an attractive reddish grey-brown colour. Plants are not self-fertile. Male and female flowers occur on separate plants: male flowers are small, round and yellow; female flowers are equally small, round and pale greenish in colour. Flowering is in late spring, around May–June.

Where to look
Native to heath and moorland, juniper is most commonly found in the more temperate regions of northern and central Europe. Its preference for acid, peaty soils makes it a likely find in and around pine forests, especially where rainfall is high and sunlight restricted.

When to look for it
The small berry-like cones are about 5 mm (¼ in) in diameter and ripen in October. However, they require two or three growing seasons in order to mature. The young cones are smooth, green and leathery, turning bluish-black when mature.

What does it taste like?
The ripe berries are highly aromatic and being composed of about 33 per cent sugar, have distinctly sweet overtones.

Often used as a flavouring in food and in gin making, juniper berries are usually left to dry after picking.

Forager's checklist

✔ Twigs are slender and smooth, often with a sheen to the bark

✔ Berries often have a white bloom

✔ Immature fruiting cones are green; black when mature

✔ Crush the berries just before use to release the flavour

Evergreen junipers thrive in peaty soils and can often be found around pine forests.

How is it used?

In Alpine regions juniper berries (cones) are an essential ingredient in many vegetable dishes, stuffings and pies. It is also an important constituent in gin. In Germany, it is used as a flavouring in sauerkraut. The fresh cabbage is fermented along with juniper berries and other spices as seasoning. Juniper berries are also often associated with strong-flavoured game, such as venison. A tea can be made from the leaves and stems; add some berries to impart more of a spicy flavour.

Caution

Although the fruit of the juniper is harmless to most people and its oil is used medicinally and as a food flavouring, excessive doses can adversely affect the kidneys, so should be avoided by anybody with kidney problems, and pregnant women.

The flowers of the juniper, which appear in later spring, are located at the base of the needle-like leaves.

Olea europaea

Olive

the oldest known cultivated tree in history • evergreen, silver-backed leaves • male and female organs on same flower • smooth bark becoming gnarled with age • green berries turning black

What is it?
An evergreen tree, slow-growing, eventually reaching 15 m (50 ft). However, olive trees are nearly always pruned in order to make harvesting the berries easier.

What to look for
The grey-green narrowly oblong leaves are silver beneath. Leaves are opposite, simple and small, about 5 cm (2 in) long, with a waxy coating and hairy undersides to minimize water loss through transpiration. Racemes of pollen-rich, creamy white (sometimes pale yellow) flowers open in spring (April–May). The bark of the olive is grey-brown, smooth when the tree is young, but becoming scaly and gnarled with age. Old trees, sometimes hundreds of years old, can have twisted, contorted, hollowed-out trunks.

Where to look
This southern European tree thrives around the entire Mediterranean region. Most often found in cultivated groves, it is drought-tolerant (once established) and will grow on nutritionally poor ground. It must, however, have full sun in order to bring its berries through to ripening.

When to look for it
Look in early autumn when fruits are still green or wait until late autumn, early winter when the fruit has turned violet-black. The colour change is triggered by an increase in oil content.

What does it taste like?
Olives are inedible until they have been processed. The olives and the resulting olive oil is sometimes flavoured with a variety of spices, herbs and other seasonings to produce a wide range of flavours. Depending on when the olive

Grown throughout the Mediterranean, olives can be picked green or left to ripen to black on the tree.

Forager's checklist

✔ Clusters of fragrant white or off-white flowers

✔ Young twigs are a fuzzy grey-green

✔ Wild olive trees have masses of spindly branches and are more shrub-like

✔ Olives need up to eight months to ripen fully

is harvested, how it has been processed, and the variety involved, these range from mild and meaty, tart and salty to sweet and fruity.

How is it used?

Olives are processed usually by being pickled with salt water, oil and a variety of flavourings. If not, they can be simply sun-dried before being eaten. Once processed, olive fruits can be used as a simple snack food, included in salads, used as a flavouring in cooked dishes, added to bread or stuffed with anything from pimentos and anchovies to almonds and garlic cloves. The fruit can also be processed to produce the magnificent olive oil, with more than half the world's production coming from just three countries – Spain, Italy and Greece.

Try it in

Olive and Orange Salad (see page 209).

Without basking in sunshine throughout a long, hot growing season, the fruit of the olive tree will not come to maturity.

Olive

Prunus dulcis syn. P. amygdalus

Sweet almond

alternate, lance-like leaves • small tree • silver-downy covering
on fruit • attractive early-spring flowers

Woodland Plants

What is it?
A small, deciduous tree with a height and
spread between 6 and 10 m (20 and 33 ft).

What to look for
The deciduous oblong to lance-like leaves are
dark green, distinctly veined and have finely
serrated edges. Apart from its edible nut kernel,
the almond has beautiful solitary flowers in late
winter or early spring, depending on location. In
more temperate zones, flowering may be
delayed until April. Flowers vary from near
white to deep pink, up to 5 cm (2 in) across,
and appear either before the leaves break or at
the same time.

Where to look
Look for this southern European tree in full sun
on the edges of wooded areas, in hedges or
rocky places near areas of cultivation. The
almond will not tolerate shade. To thrive, it also
needs moist, well-drained soil.

When to look for it
The fruit is light green, 2.5–6 cm (1–2½ in)
long, covered with a silver fuzz. It has a well-
defined groove on the side. Look for ripe fruits
in the autumn, around October. Inside the fruit is
a light-brown nut containing the much-favoured
edible almond kernel.

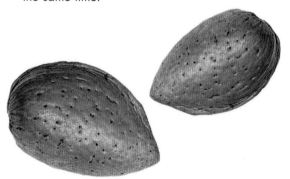

An oil extracted from the sweet almond
makes an effective moisturizer and is
also used in aromatherapy.

Forager's checklist

✔ Discard any nuts with a bitter taste

✔ Large, solitary flowers appear very early
  in the growing season

✔ Often flowers on bare wood, before leaves
  emerge

✔ Tough flesh of the fruit splits when ripe

✔ Foliage turns red in autumn

Although usually present in harmless quantities, both the leaves and seeds contain a potentially lethal toxin.

What does it taste like?
The sweet almond has a delicate, nutty flavour and attractive fragrance. If you find individual kernels that are obviously bitter when chewed and have an intense aroma, discard them immediately (see Caution below).

How is it used?
Once lightly roasted to intensify flavour, the kernel can be eaten as a snack food. It should be thoroughly chewed, however, to aid digestion. Kernels can be ground down into a fine powder for use in cakes, pastries and confections. The kernel can also be combined with water to produce almond milk or an edible oil extracted for use as a flavouring in cooking. The oil can also be used as a skin-care product and is a popular carrier oil in aromatherapy. An edible gum can also be extracted from the damaged stems of the almond tree itself.

Try it in
Arame Almond Risotto (see page 210).

Caution
The almond belongs to a genus in which most members produce a potentially deadly poison called hydrogen cyanide, a substance that gives almonds their characteristic flavour. In sweet almond, however, it is usually present in such small quantities as to do no harm. But any nut with a particularly bitter taste and intense aroma must not be eaten.

Prunus avium

Wild cherry

alternate, simple leaves • prized for its timber as well as fruit •
smooth grey-brown bark often peels • bright red fruits when ripe

What is it?
A vigorous, deciduous tree growing up to 30 m
(100 ft) high. Conical in shape when young, it
becomes more dome-shaped as it matures.

What to look for
The alternate, simple, oval- to oblong-shaped
leaves are 5–12 cm (2–5 in) long with sharply
serrated margins. Attractive and showy white
flowers appear in spring, early April and May, at
about the same time as the leaves. Flowers are
about 2.5 cm (1 in) across and grow in clusters
of up to five. Look out for the bark, which is grey-
brown to red-brown, with prominent pores,
known as 'lenticles'. The bark is smooth-textured
and often peels in strips.

Where to look
Quite commonly found in hedgerows and
woods, often in association with beech trees. It
prefers moist, well-drained soil and will tolerate
the semi-shade that you find in light woodland.
Its range is wide, taking in all of Europe, from
Scandinavia down to North Africa.

The fruit of the wild cherry is low
in acid and is most often used in
preserves and as a pie filling.

When to look for it

The wild cherry produces dark-red to near-black fruit, ripening in mid-summer. However, you will have to compete with birds and squirrels eagerly looking for their share of the tasty bonanza.

What does it taste like?

Bite into a ripe cherry and the skin splits to release a sweet to bitter-sweet explosion of flavour into your mouth. The juicy pulp of the fruit, which displays no trace of acidity, encases a single inedible cherry stone. Do not eat any cherry that tastes exceptionally bitter (see Caution below).

How is it used?

Picked straight from the tree and eaten raw, cherries make a perfect snack food. Also baked in cakes and pies, and made into preserves. To make your own cherry brandy, half-fill a sealable glass container with cherries, add sugar to taste, fill the remaining space with brandy, pop the lid into place and store for a few months away from the light.

Try it in

Cherry Clafoutis (see page 211).

Caution

The wild cherry belongs to a genus in which most members produce a potentially deadly poison called hydrogen cyanide. It is this substance that gives almonds their characteristic taste. The main parts of the wild cherry affected are the wilted leaves, stems and seeds. Do not eat any fruit that tastes exceptionally bitter.

Wild Cherry

Forager's checklist

✔ **Do not eat any fruit that is exceptionally bitter**

✔ **Leaves usually have at least eight pairs of veins**

✔ **Autumn shades of red, orange and yellow**

✔ **Spreading branches and straight main stem characterize a mature tree**

Showy displays of white flowers in early spring are an indication of a good crop of fruit to follow later.

Rosa canina

Wild rose, dog rose

fast-growing bushy shrub • stems well covered with sharp spines •
hips a rich source of vitamin C

What is it?
The wild rose is a sturdy, deciduous shrub
1–5 m (3–16 ft) high, though it can be taken
up higher if it has a suitable climbing frame,
such as a tree.

What to look for
The alternate leaves are 1–3.5 cm (½–1½ in) long
and composed of 5–7 leaflets, which are
opposite, oval-shaped and have saw-toothed
edges. Flower colour is variable, from off-white to
red or pale red, and the simple, five-petalled
blooms appear from about May/June through to
July. The numerous arching stems of this
scrambling rose are green to purple in colour,
well covered with curved prickles, which it uses to
latch on to any neighbouring plants for support.

Can be mistaken for
Hip production is common in roses and those of
the wild rose can be mistaken for any other with
the same scrambling habit and thorny stems.
Hips of other rose varieties will vary in flavour.

Where to look
Spreading by suckers, the wild rose is
commonly found throughout Europe at the
margins of woodlands, in hedgerows and on
disturbed land and scrub. It is tolerant of a wide
range of soils, but not extremely dry or wet,
poorly drained ground.

When to look for it
The fruits or hips of the wild rose follow the
flowers, developing from late summer through
autumn (August to October/November). The
attractive orange to deep-red fruits are roughly
oval-shaped and measure up to 1.5 cm (¾ in).

For the best flavour, wait until the first
frosts of autumn have touched the bush
before harvesting the hips.

The wild rose is a hardy shrub, well able to scramble up any nearby plant to help it find the best conditions.

What does it taste like?

Hips have a distinctive flavour, laced with tangy fruit overtones with underlying hints of tartness and spice.

Forager's checklist

- ✔ Flowers are 3.5–6 cm (1½–2½ in) wide in clusters of up to five blooms
- ✔ Hips become fully coloured and better flavoured after exposure to frost
- ✔ When ripe, hips should yield slightly when pressed, but not be soft or wrinkly

How is it used?

The cherry-sized rosehips are much prized for their high vitamin C content, but note that to retain the colour of the fruit and its nutritional value you should use only stainless-steel cookware. During the Second World War in Britain, rosehips were collected and used to produce rosehip syrup, an excellent substitute for unobtainable oranges. Cooked hips can be used for jams and marmalades and as a flavouring for soups and sauces, puddings, cakes and bread. Rosehip jelly is another famous dish. When dried, hips can be used as a tea, as can the dried leaves.

Caution

It is best to remove the hairy seeds before using the fruit as they can cause irritation to the digestive system.

Tilia x europaea

Lime

large, deciduous tree • famous for its linden tea • commonly used as a street tree • insect pollinated and good for wildlife

What is it?
A large, deciduous, broad-leaved tree. One of the largest trees of its type in Europe, it has been known to reach heights of approximately 45 m (150 ft).

What to look for
The cordate (heart-shaped) leaves open from red-brown buds. When fully developed, the leaves reach 5–10 cm (2–4 in) in length, starting off bright yellow, but becoming greeny-yellow with age. Flowers are very fragrant, yellow to white in colour, hanging in clusters of up to ten blooms beneath the leaves in June and early July. The bark becomes shallowly fissured with age and the base of the tree often features large, rounded outgrowths, or burls, and clusters of suckers.

Where to look
You are unlikely to find this cultivated hybrid between *T. cordata* and *T. platyphyllos* in any truly wild setting. Although it is commonly found throughout Europe, look near ornamental woods and parkland. It tolerates atmospheric pollution and partial shade, making it suitable for town/city settings, and requires moist, well-drained soil.

When to look for it
The leaves are best eaten when young and fresh, before mid-summer, while the flowers should be harvested just as they fully open – so keep an eye on them from about mid-June.

What does it taste like?
The young spring leaves have a light, mild, refreshingly sweet flavour when eaten raw, but they can be rather mucilaginous. The flowers, which are best known when made into a tea, have a strong honey aroma and flavour (but see Caution below).

Young lime leaves are delicious to eat raw and are suitable as a sandwich or salad ingredient.

Forager's checklist

✔ Finely serrated leaves

✔ Crown develops into a broadly rounded head of foliage with arching branches as it matures

✔ Fragrant, honey-scented flowers in early to mid-summer

✔ Leaves, flowers and tree sap can all be used as a food source

The flowers of the lime have been used as a traditional medicine to treat colds and other ailments.

How is it used?

Young lime leaves can be used raw in salads or as a simple sandwich filling. The most famous use, however, is in linden tea. Pick the flowers when young and leave to dry in a warm, well-ventilated room or cupboard for a few weeks. In France, the tea made from the lime is called *tilleul*. The flowers are also ground into a paste with the immature fruit of the tree to make a chocolate substitute. The sap of the tree can be used as a syrup and honey from bees that have fed on the nectar-rich flowers is regarded among the best in the world.

Try it in

Lime and Mixed Leaf Sald with Strawberries (see page 213).

Caution

Use only young, newly opened flowers for making tea. If the flowers are too old, they may have certain narcotic properties.

Urtica dioica

Stinging nettle

upright perennial • heart-shaped leaves • has been used
medicinally for more than 2,000 years • leaves covered
with stinging hairs

What is it?
This clump-forming perennial plant can reach
heights of 4 m (13 ft) in tropical regions of the
world. In Europe, however, where it proliferates,
it is more usually 60–120 cm (2–4 ft).

What to look for
This perennial plant produces pointed cordate
(heart-shaped) or egg-shaped, opposite leaves
with rounded, serrated edges. Dull green leaves
are about 5–15 cm (2–6 in) long and less than
half this wide. The nettle's flowers are tiny,
growing in dangling catkins, light green or
greeny-yellow over a long period between June
and September.

Where to look
The stinging nettle has become naturalized
all over the world. It is an adaptable plant,
growing on disturbed, natural and cultivated
land such as hedgerows and the margins
of woodland.

When to look for it
It is crucial to harvest the leaves at the right time
of year. Although the nettle is in leaf from March
to November, pick the leaves when they are
young and fresh – some say that the beginning
of June is the cut-off point. After this time they
become coarse, bitter and, as autumn looms,

Eat only the young leaves of the
stinging nettle; older leaves contain
particles that can irritate the kidneys.

Forager's checklist

✔ Nettles reproduce from seed and by
  sending out a long root from which new
  plants grow

✔ Stems are four-sided rather than round

✔ Leaves and stems both covered in
  stinging hairs

✔ Commonly found all over the world

increasingly gritty. It is best to pick just the top 15–20 cm (6–8 in) of the plant, wearing gloves whenever handling the raw leaves or stems.

What does it taste like?
Nettles, either cooked as a vegetable or dried and made into a tea, are rather bland, though highly nutritious, and are best prepared with plenty of seasoning and tasty ingredients.

How is it used?
Cooking or thoroughly drying nettle leaves and stems neutralizes the stinging properties of the plant. The young spring leaves and top few centimetres (inches) of the stems can be treated much like spinach – washed and then cooked for a few minutes in just the droplets of water that stick to the leaves. Served as greens with pepper and butter, they are an easily digestible food (though slightly laxative in effect), high in iron and vitamins A and C. The young leaves can be dried and the crushed leaves can be added to more flavoursome teas for a tonic effect. The young nettle shoots can also be brewed into a beer, taking only about a week from picking.

Caution
The sting of a nettle is not unlike that of a bee and the effects can last from a few hours to more than a day, depending on individual sensitivity. In rare cases, medical help may be needed if the reaction is extreme. Eating nettles can lower both blood pressure and heart rate.

Stinging Nettle

Both male and female plants are required if seed is to be produced and plants are noted for attracting wildlife.

Vaccinium myrtillus

Bilberry, whortleberry

vigorous, low-growing shrub • oval-shaped leaves • valued as a
food plant and for its medicinal qualities • delicious in tarts and jams

What is it?
A low-growing deciduous shrub reaching a
maximum 20–30 cm (8–12 in). Clump-forming
and potentially invasive in good, fertile ground.

The sweet fruit of the bilberry is
suitable for drying and can be used
much as you would currants.

What to look for
The bilberry produces a mass of upright stems,
with oval, bright green, alternate leaves with
slightly serrated edges. Leaves are 1–2.5 cm
(½–1 in) long. The pinkish or greeny-pink
flowers appear between April and June –
usually solitary (though sometimes in pairs),
urn-shaped and about 5 mm (¼ in) long.

Where to look
Preferring the temperate climate of northern
Europe or the cooler temperatures at higher
altitudes in the south, look for bilberry bushes
sheltering under the canopy of tall trees in
mature woodland, as well as on moorland
and heath.

When to look for it
The highly prized edible berry follows the
flowers, and the spherical dark-blue fruits ripen
during the summer months of July to September.

What does it taste like?
The raw berries have a sweet taste, though there
are definite acid overtones. Once cooked, the
acid flavour disappears, leaving a delicious
sweetness behind.

How is it used?

The bilberry has been valued as a delicacy for hundreds of years. Its berries can be enjoyed raw. Cooked bilberries, however, are used as a traditional filling for pies and tarts, as well as for making into jelly and conserves. They can also be fermented to make wine. As an alternative, the berries become currant-like when dried and a tea can be made from its dried leaves. In France since the mid-20th century, bilberries have been prescribed to help protect the vision of people suffering from diabetes – they are also thought to improve night vision generally – and in Italy research indicates that they help lower blood cholesterol levels.

Try it in

Bilberry Pie (see page 214).

This shrub grows in sandy or loamy soil that is moist but well drained. It does well even on highly acid soils.

Forager's checklist

- ✔ Bright-green, serrated leaves
- ✔ Berries small, about 1 cm (½ in) in diameter
- ✔ Prefers sandy or loamy, well-drained soils
- ✔ Will not tolerate a maritime exposure
- ✔ Twigs multi-branched and acutely angled

Bilberry

WOODLAND FUNGI

The prospect of the good eating to follow a successful woodland forage is only part of the allure. What better pleasure can there be than to feel the deep-piled carpet of fallen leaves beneath your boots, to smell that heady aroma of dampness and soil and decay, and then to spy your objective. Perhaps you've found the vase-shaped cap and bright orange-yellow colour of a wonderful chanterelle, or a larger-than-life cep, also known as a penny bun because of its glazed bun-like cap? With luck, a morning's foraging can net you a basketful of mouth-watering fungi, food to grace the best restaurant in town – and yours for free.

Auricularia auricularia-judae

Jew's ear

young specimens make the best eating • commonly used in Asian cuisine • a mineral-rich species • can be found any time of the year

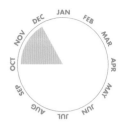

What is it?
A very distinctive bracket fungus, shaped like an ear, approximately 5 cm (2 in) across. Usually gregarious (found in groups).

What to look for
As its common name implies, this fungus looks distinctly like a disembodied ear growing out of the side of a tree. A warm-brown colour and gelatinous and fleshy to the touch when moist, it becomes darker and harder and more violet as it dries out. When young, the fungus has a predominantly smooth, cup-like shape, elongating as it matures and developing more of a wrinkled interior.

Can be mistaken for
Other bracket fungi can be mistaken for Jew's ear. Tripe fungus (*Auricularia mesenterica*) is hairier and is more commonly found on elm; witch's butter (*Exidia glandulosa*) is darker, almost black, and is often found growing on oak.

Where to look
Common throughout Europe, this species of fungus is always associated with dead or dying wood. Its common name is thought to be a corruption of 'Judas's ear' who, the story goes,

hanged himself from an elder tree – and it is the elder you should look for when foraging, as it is the most favoured growing site. Beech and sycamore trees also play host to this fungus.

When to look for it
Unusually, the Jew's ear fungus can be found throughout the year, whenever the weather is mild. The peak months for collecting are October, November and into December. February to May can also be good foraging months.

When mature, the fruiting body is approximately the same size and shape as a human ear.

Forager's checklist

✔ Colour changes from reddish-brown to violet as it dries

✔ Usually found in a group of specimens

✔ Flesh becomes slightly translucent when dry

✔ Most commonly found in spring and autumn/winter

✔ Wash the fungus well before preparing it for the pot

Jew's Ear

What does it taste like?

A pleasant, mild flavour. If cooked properly, young specimens also have good *al dente* qualities without being chewy. This fungus is probably more appreciated for the texture it lends dishes than for its flavour.

How is it used?

Containing good amounts of minerals such as potassium, calcium and magnesium, Jew's ear makes a healthy dietary addition. Do not undercook, however, or results may be too chewy. To help tenderize, slice the fungus thinly and then add to a stock and cook for at least 20 minutes. Alternatively, gently fry the thinly sliced fungus in butter, seasoned to taste with salt, pepper, garlic and onions. Once dried and powdered, it stores well for later use as a thickening agent in cooking.

This fungus is most often found growing on dead wood – principally that of elder, but also other broad-leaved trees.

Boletus edulis

Cep, penny bun

highly prized for flavour and texture • has the appearance of a
glazed bun • broad stem bulging towards the bottom • can be
dried for storage

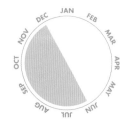

Woodland Fungi

What is it?
A large fungus with variable cap colour – from
light brown, through chestnut brown verging on
red – growing on a stem 7–25 cm (3–10 in)
high. On a mature specimen, the cap can
measure 7–30 cm (3–12 in) in diameter.

What to look for
The cap of the young cep is distinctly convex,
becoming flatter as it ages. Under the thick and
fleshy cap, the arrangement of gills typical of
the field mushroom (see pages 104–105) are
absent, replaced by pores making it look
somewhat like a fine-textured sponge (white on
young specimens, yellow on older ones). The
stem is brown, streaked with white, with a net-
like honeycomb pattern near the cap.

Can be mistaken for
Look out for the dramatically named devil's
bolete (*Boletus satanus*). This poisonous fungus
can cause violent sickness no matter how little
is eaten. This fungus nearly always grows
singly near oak or beech trees; its cap remains
convex even on mature specimens. The pores
under the cap and the stem are red. The flesh
turns slightly blue when cut and has an
unpleasant, rotting smell.

The thick, fleshy, convex cap and
bulbous stem make the very popular
cep one of the easier fungi to identify.

Where to look

Found throughout Europe, most often in association with conifers and broad-leaved trees, especially beech. Concentrate your search on the edges of woods or clearings or in grassland where trees are also present.

When to look for it

Can be found any time between June and December, peaking in September and October.

What does it taste like?

Regarded as one of the very finest tasting of all the fungus species, it has both a delicious nutty, meaty flavour and a firm texture.

How is it used?

Known as the 'cep' in France, but probably more recognizable to most people by its Italian name, *porcini*, this is one of the most distinguished of edible fungi. The number of recipes that feature this fungus are too numerous to mention, but the more obvious ones, apart from simply eating them raw (delicious), include pickling young specimens whole, frying them with bacon in olive oil, using them as a flavouring in Bolognese sauce, teaming them with paprika, garlic and onions, and charcoal-grilling them as an accompaniment to meats. Most people know the cep, or porcini, in its dried form, which is available in supermarkets and delicatessens around the world.

Try it in

Cep Pancakes (see page 212).

Yellow-brown, sponge-rubber-looking spores under the cap replace the gills normally associated with fungi.

Forager's checklist

- ✔ Sweet-smelling
- ✔ Check for insect infestation before eating
- ✔ Flesh does not discolour when bruised
- ✔ Grows beneath both conifers and broad-leaved trees
- ✔ Cap feels tacky when wet
- ✔ Base of stem is very swollen

Cantharellus cibarius

Chanterelle

bright, conspicuous fungus • typically vase-shaped • usually tough
if rehydrated • stem and cap similar colours

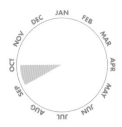

Woodland Fungi

What is it?
This ground-growing fungus is unmissable to collectors due to its bright yellow to orange-yellow colouring and its vase- or funnel-shaped form. Standing 1.5–9 cm (¾–3½ in) high, its cap is 2.5–10 cm (1–4 in) across.

What to look for
The chanterelle's overall colour fades slightly with age, and the stem may be a slightly lighter than the cap. Apart from colour, one of the most striking characteristics of the chanterelle (girolle in France) is the deeply folded false gills under the cap, running down the stem, making the fungus look almost architectural in appearance. The flesh is a pale yellow and does not change colour when cut or bruised.

Can be mistaken for
The rare but poisonous Jack O'Lantern (*Omphalotus olearius*) can be mistaken for the chanterelle. Similar in size and overall colour, the Jack O'Lantern is found in large groups growing at the base of live trees or on rotting stumps. The gills of this fungus glow faintly green at night.

Where to look
Found throughout Europe, it is best to search for chanterelles on the ground beneath broad-leaved trees (beech and oak especially) as well as conifers. Prefers a reasonably open, sloping site where groundcover plants are scarce, so also keep an eye out for them adjacent to woodland paths.

When to look for it
The main collecting time for the chanterelle is in the autumn (September and October), until the first frosts arrive, and also in mid-summer (around July).

Popularly eaten throughout Europe, the chanterelle can often be found in shops and on market stalls.

The attractively vaulted gills of the chanterelle appear to grow directly from the stem, which has no ring.

Forager's checklist

✔ **Try looking underneath deciduous hedgerows**

✔ **Surface of the stem feels dry and smooth**

✔ **Resistant to insect infestation**

✔ **Cap can have a wavy, undulating edge**

✔ **When growing in a group, stems are often curved and sometimes joined together**

✔ **Flesh is thick and firm**

What does it taste like?

Up there in the elite class of edible fungi, the chanterelle is said to be 'the perfect taste of the wild mushroom'. It has a slightly peppery flavour and smells distinctly of sweet apricots.

How is it used?

Unfortunately for those who cannot get out into the woods foraging for themselves, the chanterelle is a fungus best prepared and eaten fresh. They can be dried, but usually taste leathery and tough when reconstituted. Nor do they freeze well. Try eating chanterelles raw, especially young specimens, or slice larger ones thinly and fry them seasoned to taste or as an accompaniment to scrambled eggs or as an omelette filling.

Try it in

Fettucine with Chanterelles (see page 215).

Laetiporus sulphureus

Chicken of the woods

easily recognizable fungus • found growing from a wide range of trees • older specimens are often tough • recurs in same place year after year

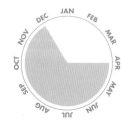

Woodland Fungi

What is it?
A large bracket fungus, bright yellow when young, fading to pale yellow and eventually white. Each spreads out into a fan and can be up to 60 cm (24 in) across at its widest point, and 2.5–3.5 cm (1–1½ in) thick.

What to look for
This fungus grows in large clusters of overlapping fans on living trees as well as decaying wood. The upper surface of each one is usually smooth or slightly rough in texture, with bright-orange, curved edges. The under surface has fine pores giving a sponge-like effect and is lemon-yellow, fading to white with age and becoming brittle. Flesh is meaty and soft, yellow in colour, when young; becoming paler (almost white) and powdery with age.

Where to look
You can find chicken of the woods growing from a wide range of trees, including yew, beech, oak, sweet chestnut, eucalyptus, cherry and willow. Found throughout Europe, its preference is for older trees or fallen wood or decaying stumps, so concentrate your search in more established woodland rather than new plantings.

When to look for it
Apart from the depths of winter, you can find chicken of the woods throughout the rest of the year (April to December), though you are likely to have most luck around June and then again in the autumn (September and October).

What does it taste like?
Not a favourite with everybody, this fungus smells strongly of, well, fungus. The clue to its flavour, however, lies in its common name – once cooked it looks and tastes very much like chicken. It even has a similar flaky texture.

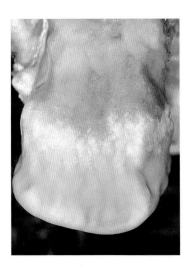

The texture of the flesh as well as its flavour give this woodland species its well-described common name.

How is it used?

Never eat chicken of woods raw, as it can cause an unpleasant stomach upset (see Caution below). To be safe, it is best to choose young specimens for the pot – the taste is superior and the flesh softer. Older fungi can become bitter and tough. Blanching before cooking helps remove any bitterness. Grilling or shallow frying slices of the flesh is the usual method of cooking, seasoned to taste. It does not dry well, but can be successfully frozen raw.

Try it in

Chicken of the Woods Ragout (see page 216).

Caution

Chicken of the woods is a popular edible fungus, but it should always be thoroughly cooked to minimize the possibility of stomach upsets.

Chicken of the woods can be found growing on both dead and living wood, especially that of old oak trees.

Forager's checklist

✔ Highly distinctive fungus, unlikely to be confused with any other

✔ Always cook it well before eating

✔ Fans of growing fungus take up a lot of water and can exude drops of a pale-coloured liquid

✔ Colour of fans likely to be more muted if growing in direct sunlight

✔ Suede-texture on upper surfaces

Leccinum versipelle

Orange birch bolete

widely distributed • firm, flavoursome flesh • distinctive orange
cap • strikingly large fungus

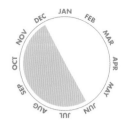

What is it?
This very large fungus stands up to 25 cm
(10 in) high; the cap is usually orange but can
also be reddish-pink. Can be a sizeable 25 cm
(10 in) across.

What to look for
The cap of this fungus is usually convex or
shield-shaped, becoming flatter as it ages, often
with scales in the centre. It is slightly downy in
appearance when young, becoming smooth as
it matures. The stem is white or a mottled grey
with dark-brown scales. The pores beneath the
cap are very small, at first dark grey, but
becoming lighter in colour – white to buff. The
flesh of the stipe (or stem) turns blue-green and
then black when exposed to the air after cutting.

Can be mistaken for
The related *Leccinum scabrum* can be mistaken
for the orange birch bolete. You find this edible
fungus most often under birch trees, often in
association with *L. versipelle*, but its cap is
brown in colour rather than orange and,
more significantly, the flesh of the stem does
not obviously change colour when cut and
exposed to the air.

Where to look
As you can assume from its common name,
it is best to look for this fungus under birch
trees, especially trees growing on open heathland and scrub, as well as under conifers and
with bracken.

When to look for it
Can be found any time between June and
December, peaking in August, September
and October.

Another name for this fungus, sponge
cap, accurately describes its large,
fleshy, orange-coloured cap.

What does it taste like?

This fungus has a good nutty flavour and a pleasant odour. Though not in the same league as the cep (see pages 60–61), its flesh is firmer and it makes a worthwhile addition to a meal featuring mixed fungi.

How is it used?

It is best to remove most of the stem of older specimens before preparing for the pot. In any case, always remove the stem scales. This versatile fungus can then be used as an ingredient in soups or you can fry or casserole it. You can also dry or pickle it for later use. Try cooking the thinly sliced cap in olive oil with garlic and onions. Season to taste, add a generous knob of butter and serve on toast.

Try it in

Bolete Pie (see page 217).

Forager's checklist

- ✔ **Resistant to insect infestation**
- ✔ **Can weigh up to 1 kg (2 lb)**
- ✔ **Stem flesh changes colour markedly when cut**
- ✔ **Cap flesh turns nearly black when cooked**
- ✔ **Look for the birch tree association**

Orange Birch Bolete

The dark-coloured scales covering the stem of the orange birch bolete are a key identifying feature of the species.

Pleurotus ostreatus

Oyster mushroom

fan-shaped, overlapping growth • widely distributed • parasitic on live trees • available year-round

Woodland Fungi

What is it?
A fan-shaped, tree-growing fungus. Each fan can be up to 20 cm (8 in) wide and 1.5–2.5 cm (¾–1 in) thick. The stem, if present, is often 'eccentric' (off-centre). The fungus varies from white to off-white and blue-grey to beige.

What to look for
Its name 'oyster', refers to its appearance, not its flavour. The cap of the young oyster mushroom is convex, but tends to become flatter, or even slightly concave, as it ages. At its edges, the cap slightly undulates and curves under towards the gills. When present, the stem is white and slightly woolly where it joins the wood of the tree. The gills are usually white, becoming yellower with age.

Can be mistaken for
The likely fungi to cause identification problems here are non-poisonous, though not necessarily good to eat. The most similar in terms of appearance and habit is the branched oyster mushroom (*Pleurotus cornucopiae*), which is usually found growing on dead elm wood. It is not particularly good eating, but it should not cause problems if cooked well.

Where to look
A commonly found fungus in the cooler, more temperate areas of Europe, usually, but not exclusively, growing on the trunks of dead hardwood trees (sometimes even on fence posts). Beech trees are a popular host for this species of fungus. It is only rarely found in association with conifers.

When to look for it
Apart from the height of mid-summer you can find the oyster mushroom year-round, though autumn and winter (especially December) are the peak seasons.

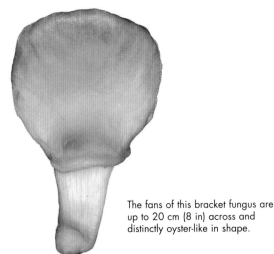

The fans of this bracket fungus are up to 20 cm (8 in) across and distinctly oyster-like in shape.

What does it taste like?

Depending on when you pick this fungus, its taste can vary from mild to strong, sometimes sweet-tasting, sometimes with a subtle hint of liquorice. Its texture is also variable and is often meatier if picked in the winter months.

How is it used?

Since the oyster mushroom is amenable to cultivation, it is becoming increasingly common to find this fungus on the shelves of specialist delicatessens, greengrocers and supermarkets – though foragers would claim that cultivated specimens lack the flavour of the wild-gathered ones. The oyster mushroom does not dry well. The smaller specimens are usually tastier and more tender. Remove any of the stem and then slice, cover in seasoned breadcrumbs and deep-fry. Alternatively, sauté in butter or olive oil on a gentle heat with garlic.

The gills of the oyster mushroom are white or yellow in colour, while the cap is more grey-blue.

Caution

An allergic reaction is possible from inhaling the spores of the oyster mushroom.

Forager's checklist

✔ Eccentric stem

✔ Grows on wood, not the ground

✔ The flesh has a pleasant smell

✔ Found in clusters of overlapping fans

✔ Check for insect infestation before cooking

Sparassis crispa

Brain fungus

grows in the same place, season after season • large, complex structure • becomes tougher with age • dries successfully

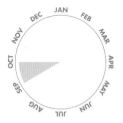

Woodland Fungi

What is it?
A large, round fungus similar in appearance to a cauliflower, brain or sponge. The stem is often not apparent, being deeply buried, or is completely absent, and the fruiting body itself measures 12–40 cm (5–16 in) across.

What to look for
This often solitary fungus is composed of densely packed, convoluted, flattened branches growing from a central stem, producing a rounded head of material. Its colour is variable, depending on age – starting off creamy, off-white to yellow and becoming darker tan or brown all over. The colour change is especially apparent on the edges of the branches. The flesh is pale to white.

Can be mistaken for
A similar-looking species is *Grifola frondosa*, which also forms a similar rounded, cauliflower-shaped head of material, but the segments are flatter and more fan-shaped in appearance, and it is principally associated with oak. No harm will be done if it is picked in error, as this species is also edible.

Where to look
Widely distributed throughout Europe, the brain fungus is nearly always found on the stumps of dead pine trees or on the ground near living pine trees. It is occasionally found in association with other conifers, but not broad-leaved trees.

When to look for it
You have only a narrow window of opportunity to harvest the brain fungus, as it fruits in mid-autumn (around September and October). Where the climate is mild, you may find them fruiting into early winter.

Looking at this specimen, it is easy to see how its other common name came about – cauliflower fungus.

Before cooking, cut the fungus up into chunks and wash thoroughly to remove insects and debris.

Forager's checklist

✔ Fragrant-smelling rather than earthy
✔ Stem is often buried and is tough and root-like
✔ Found exclusively in conifer woods
✔ Limited fruiting season
✔ Grows on wood and on the ground
✔ Flesh of young specimens is brittle

What does it taste like?
Older specimens of the brain fungus become tough and bitter-tasting. Young specimens are delicious – the flesh has rather a fragrant, spicy odour and a pleasant taste of hazelnuts.

How is it used?
Because of its design, you need to clean this fungus thoroughly before cooking to remove debris – especially pine needles, insects and soil – trapped into its convolutions. It is better to use a brush to do this. It will stand up to washing if it is very dirty, but then dry it thoroughly before cooking. Only collect young, light-coloured specimens as they have the best flavour. After slicing or cutting into rough chunks, the fungus can be sautéd, baked or dipped in a beer batter and deep-fried. Its nutty flavour also makes it an excellent addition to casseroles and soups.

Xerocomus badius

Bolete, bay bolete

stem has a streaky appearance • widely distributed • flesh
changes colour when cut • dries successfully

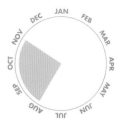

Woodland Fungi

What is it?
Standing up to 15 cm (6 in) high and with
a cap 7–15 cm (3–6 in) across, this large
fungus has a downy, velvety appearance when
immature, but the cap turns a distinctive, smooth
bay brown or warm chestnut as it matures.

What to look for
The cap is distinctly convex, slightly undulating
at the edges. Beneath the cap is a fine network
of yellow pores, turning blue-green as soon as
they are bruised. The flesh is firm and pale,
turning faintly blue when exposed to the air after
being cut or broken. The stipe (stem) is brown,
sturdy (but not bulbous), about 2.5 cm (1 in) in
diameter and covered with threads, giving it a
streaky appearance.

Can be mistaken for
You can mistake the edible cep (see pages
60–61) for the bay bolete. If in doubt, look for
the net pattern on the stem that signifies the cep.
The dotted-stem bolete (*Boletus erythropus*) is
another potential lookalike. Again, look to the
stem, as this species has a bulbous, yellow stem
with, as you might guess from its common
name, red dots. It causes stomach disorders,
even if well cooked, and so is best left alone.

Where to look
The best locations to look for this widely
distributed fungus is in pine (particularly Scot's
pine – *Pinus sylvestris*) and spruce forests,

This widely distributed woodland
species can be found in both
coniferous and broad-leaved forests.

Forager's checklist

✔ Bruised specimens can leave a blue stain on your hands

✔ Not prone to insect infestation

✔ Found in large groups and as isolated individuals

✔ Cap becomes flatter with age

✔ Grows best in an acid soil

✔ Cap downy when young, becoming smooth later

The bolete has a curved, non-bulbous stem, warm yellow-brown in colour, and marked with distinct streaks.

although it is also found associated with broad-leaves, such as oak, beach and sweet chestnuts.

When to look for it

The best time to find the bay bolete is in the autumn after a prolonged damp period during the summer. Look out for it from late summer onwards (August to November).

What does it taste like?

The bay bolete has a subtle, delicate flavour and aroma, and although tasty it is not particularly distinctive.

How is it used?

This versatile fungus lends itself to inclusion in many dishes. First, carefully clean away any leaf clutter or soil. Check for insect infestation, although this is rare with this species. You will probably need to discard the stem as being too coarse and tough. Casseroles, stews and soups are obvious uses for the bay bolete, or you can slice it thinly and fry it gently in butter, seasoned to taste, and use it as a vegetable in its own right. It can also be dried successfully and reconstituted and used as a food flavouring at a later date.

Try it in

Bolete Pie (see page 217).

RIVERSIDE PLANTS

The sight and sound of flowing water are a tonic, soothing the soul and stilling the mind. But the presence of moving water does more than this — it provides the constant moisture so loved by some of the tastiest food plants available in nature's pantry. These include sweet cicely, with its intense flavour of aniseed; coriander and parsley, the background flavours and aromas of so many of our best-loved dishes; as well as alexanders, which fell out of favour only when the celery we know today was introduced.

Barbarea vulgaris

Winter cress, yellow rocket

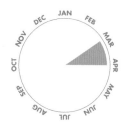

upright biennial or perennial • bright yellow flowers in mid-spring
• can be eaten raw or cooked • widely distributed

Riverside Plants

What is it?
A clump-forming biennial or perennial plant that can reach 35–40 cm (14–16 in) high, with flowering stems reaching 1 m (3 ft) high.

What to look for
The leaves of winter cress are alternate, shiny, dark green and toothed. Lower leaves are lobed, 5–20 cm (2–8 in) long, with the terminal lobe having a broadly cordate base; upper leaves are smaller and less lobed. The four-petalled flowers are bright yellow and open in the spring through to early summer (April–June). They are produced in elongated clusters on glabrous stems standing well above the lower rosettes of leaves.

Can be mistaken for
The flowers of winter cress can be confused with those of wild mustard (*Brassica kaber*) and wild radish (*Raphanus raphanistrum*).

Where to look
Winter cress can be found on pasture land, by drainage ditches and on waste and disturbed ground, usually in association with running water. It prefers moist, but well-drained, fertile, slightly acid soil. It is native to Eurasia and is naturalized throughout the temperate regions of the northern hemisphere.

To encourage year-round availability of the leaves, remove the flowering stems before they develop buds.

Forager's checklist

✔ Serrated, dark-green, lobed leaves in basal rosettes

✔ Tall, smooth, hairless stems of bright yellow flowers

✔ Thrives in damp, well-drained soil

✔ Popular wildlife plant

✔ Grows from a taproot and has a network of fibrous roots

When to look for it

Harvest this plant in early spring when the fresh young leaves can be added to salads or cooked (see below). However, where the winters are mild, the leaves are available year round. Prolonged leaf production is possible by removing the flowering stems before the flowers open. You can then pick the new outer leaves as they are produced.

What does it taste like?

The leaves of winter cress have a distinctly hot, pleasantly bitter flavour, making them the perfect antidote to the milder, sometimes insipid flavours of many commercially produced salad leaves.

How is it used?

The young leaves are the ones to go for. They can be used raw, finely chopped, as a salad ingredient or, along with some of the older leaves, cooked in a little boiling water, much as you would spinach. Less usual is to use the flowering stems. Select young stems of winter cress before the flowers have opened and lightly boil or steam them.

Try it in

Winter Cress Salad (see page 218)

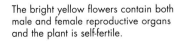
The bright yellow flowers contain both male and female reproductive organs and the plant is self-fertile.

Calluna vulgaris

Heather

tenacious evergreen shrub • dense and compact growth •
mat-forming and can be invasive • good autumn/winter colour

The blooms of heather are solitary and
are arranged towards the ends of the
flower-bearing stems.

Riverside Plants

What is it?
A low, mat-forming, evergreen undershrub or
dwarf shrub. As broad as it is tall, it may grow
60–100 cm (2–3 ft) high.

What to look for
Heather is native to northwest Europe where,
given the right conditions, it can form invasive
mats of groundcover. Leaves are opposite,
small, almost scale-like, usually not more than
2.5 cm (1 in) long, mid-green in summer. In
autumn, the evergreen foliage takes on hints of
red, yellow or bronze. Flowers open late
summer through to early autumn (July to
September), forming purple spikes of bell-
shaped blooms.

Where to look
An adaptable shrub, able to also live on quite
dry ground, heather thrives in damp acid soils
found beside rivers and on bogs and moors. It
will tolerate shade or full sun and it will also
thrive in coastal growing conditions, with its wind
and salt. It does best in nutritionally poor soil.

When to look for it
Keep an eye on heather during the summer and
gather the stems when the flowers are fully open.

Forager's checklist

✔ Leaves arranged on shoots in four rows
✔ Patterns of growth vary depending on conditions
✔ Flowers rosy to purple-pink, about 5 mm (¼ in) long
✔ Seeds ripen in late autumn
✔ Spring-flowering heather is *Erica*, not *Calluna*

The flowers can be intoxicatingly fragrant and so full of nectar that honey produced by bees feeding on them is among the best in the world.

What does it taste like?
The flowers have to be processed before the flavour becomes apparent.

How is it used?
The edible parts of heather are the flower heads and stems, which, after drying, are made into a tea. This traditional drink was reputed to have been a favourite of Scottish poet Robert Burns. Traditionally, the young shoots were once used as a flavouring in the production of ale instead of hops, and heather flowers blended with honey can be used as flavouring for mead-type drinks.

Where conditions allow, heather will grow to cover all available ground, thus forming a continuous mat of foliage.

Heather

Coriandrum sativum

Coriander

delicate-looking annual plant • not completely frost hardy •
leaves, seeds and root can be used in cooking • probably the
most widely used spice in the world

What is it?
Don't be fooled by the delicate fronds of this
annual – it can be tenacious. Reaching a height
of 60–90 cm (24–36 in) and with a spread of
30–60 cm (12–24 in), it will tolerate light frosts,
but does not like excessive heat and humidity.

What to look for
Coriander has two distinctly different leaf types.
The lobed lower leaves are opposite and
2.5–5 cm (1–2 in) across, while the upper leaves
are finely dissected (linear lobed) and could be
mistaken for those of a fern. Coriander belongs
to the same family as the carrot, which also
produces fern-like foliage. Umbels of white or
pink flowers appear in June and July, followed by
seed that ripens between August and September.

Where to look
Coriander likes a well-drained, light, sandy soil,
preferably in dappled shade. Since 'wild'
coriander is likely to be an escapee from
cultivation, the best place to look is on waste
ground adjacent to arable land, and often near
running water, where it can obtain a ready
supply of moisture. Coriander is native to the
Mediterranean region but is found throughout
temperate Europe.

When to look for it
Coriander has two periods of interest for the
forager. In late spring and early summer, the
fern-like leaves, known as cilantro, are ready
for picking. If you intend to revisit the plant later
for its crop of seeds, pick just the leaves you
need for immediate use, thus ensuring the plant's
continued vigour. Then in late summer (August to
September), the plant will be dead and you can
return for the seeds we all know as 'coriander'.

The edges of coriander leaves are
serrated, but irregularly so. These
are the lower, lobed leaves.

What does it taste like?

The lacy, fern-like cilantro leaves are full of tangy, aromatic flavour and have a fresh, distinctive aroma. The seeds only take on their fragrant, aromatic flavour when dried. Note, the fresh seeds are described as having an extremely unpleasant, vaguely nauseous aroma. This disappears as the seeds dry.

How is it used?

Coriander was cultivated in ancient Egypt and has been part of our culinary heritage for 5,000 years. The foliage (cilantro) can be picked fresh from the plant as required and used as a garnish and flavouring with spicy salads, soups, meat dishes (especially pork) and, of course, curries. It is important in cuisines as varied as Chinese, Latin American and North African and can be frozen if necessary. Dried coriander seeds are indispensable in many dishes from the Middle East, Mediterranean, Europe and India. Ground into a fine powder, coriander seeds are also used as a flavouring for cakes and confectioneries. The root can also be dried and powdered for use as a food flavouring.

Try it in

Coriander and Black Bean Soup (see page 223).

Forager's checklist

✔ Stems round and grooved
✔ A profusion of flowers makes the plant distinctive
✔ Seeds mature in round, yellow-brown pods
✔ Unripe seeds are bitter-tasting
✔ Leaves are strongly aromatic

Coriander seeds develop once the flowers die and are ready for collecting between August and September.

Fragaria vesca

Wild strawberry

spreading, potentially invasive perennial • smaller fruit than
cultivated varieties • fruit requires a long ripening period •
leaves, fruit and roots can all be used

What is it?
A low-growing, perennial plant that spreads by
runners, by seed or by division. Reaching only
about 30 cm (12 in) high, and with a spread of
25 cm (10 in), this robust little plant can quickly
produce mats of locally invasive groundcover.

What to look for
The leaf stalks of the wild strawberry and its
flower stems are a greenish-red/purple and can
be densely covered in hairs. The leaves are
compound, composed of three ovate (egg-
shaped) leaflets with serrated edges. The longer,
middle leaflet has a V-shaped base. The five-
petalled, white flowers, 3–15 blooms held on
stems up to 25 cm (10 in) long, open over a long
period between May and October, and usually
stand proud of the leaves. The wild strawberry is
widespread throughout temperate Europe.

Where to look
This plant requires moist but well-drained ground
and can be found in a range of soil types,
including heavy clay. Tolerating light, open
shade or full sun, it can be found in a range of
diverse habitats, including woodland edges,
grass and scrubland, streamside banks, and
open ground adjacent to paths.

When to look for it
Everybody loves the strawberry plant for its
bright red clusters of fruit with prominently
protruding seeds. Look carefully beneath the
leaves between late June and, depending on
the first frosts, up to November. You may
have to compete with the local bird and slug
populations for the sweet strawberries.

What does it taste like?
The wild strawberry produces smaller fruit than
cultivated varieties, but its flavour is sweet and

The three-lobed, serrated-edged leaves
of the wild strawberry are a distinctive
feature of the plant.

intense, often far superior to the beautiful-looking though rather insipid offerings available in most supermarkets.

How is it used?
The ripe fruit are most often enjoyed eaten fresh and raw, either as a snack food or as part of a fresh fruit salad. Or you can add them to your breakfast bowl of cereal. You can purée the berries and use them as a sweet, fruity sauce for other fruit dishes or as a flavouring for ice cream. The berries can be made into delicious preserves. The leaves – fresh or dried – can be used as a refreshing tea substitute. Use young leaves and leave them to dry for a few days. Finally, the rhizome (root) of the plant can be used as a coffee substitute.

Try it in
Wild Strawberry Ice Cream (see page 219).

Forager's checklist

- ✔ Leaves have prominent veins
- ✔ Fruits are about 1.5 cm (¾ in) in diameter
- ✔ Always check under the leaves for extra-ripe berries
- ✔ Flowers held on stalks above the leaves
- ✔ Needs a source of moisture to make the berries swell

Wild Strawberry

Insects, such as bees, flies, butterflies and moths, are essential for the successful pollination of the strawberry.

Bog myrtle, sweet gale

bushy deciduous shrub • male and female catkins on separate
plants • flowers open on bare stems • can be used fresh or dried

What is it?
A small- to medium-growing deciduous shrub
1.5–2 m (5–6½ ft) high with a spread of about
1 m (3 ft).

What to look for
The simple leaves are alternate, narrow and
obovate (egg-shaped, but with the narrower end
at the base), and the edges are toothed only
towards the tip. They are fragrant, blue-green
(the upper surfaces being darker than the lower
ones) and about 2.5–7 cm (1–3 in) long. The
bark is reddish-brown with lighter lenticels
(pores), becoming greyer with age. Short catkins
of yellow flowers appear in spring (March–May)
before the leaves are on the branches, and
these are followed by seeds that ripen in late
summer (August–September).

Where to look
This water-loving plant grows in bogs, on
marshland, wet heaths and other areas
where the soil is permanently moist or wet,
predominantly in northern Europe. It prefers
full sun or the dappled, open shade found on
the sunny edge of a wood.

When to look for it
Pick the leaves of bog myrtle throughout the
growing season, from late May onwards, until
the leaves drop in autumn. If you want the
flowers as a flavouring, then March–May is the
best time to look. The season of interest for the
berries is the late summer (August–September)

The flowers are either male or female
and plants are single-sexed, so both
types must be present for fertilization.

Forager's checklist

✔ Stems and leaves are fragrant when bruised or crushed

✔ Aroma intensifies when leaves are dried

✔ Flowers grow on the previous year's wood

✔ Twigs are slender and dark brown in colour

Bog Myrtle

What does it taste like?

The fruits and leaves are fragrant and aromatic, an aroma that is largely mirrored in the taste. If you use older leaves, however, the taste can be astringent and slightly bitter.

How is it used?

The leaves of bog myrtle were used to flavour beer in Germany, Belgium and Great Britain long before the introduction of hops. Use the leaves as you would bay leaves in soups, sauces and stews, removing them before serving. The leaves, once dried and crushed, make a very pleasant tea substitute, while you can use the dried berries as a spice.

Caution

This plant contains a chemical agent capable of inducing miscarriages. Do not eat this plant if you are pregnant or suspect that you may be.

Given favourable conditions, bog myrtle will form dense thickets. Flowers appear on wood that is one year old.

Myrrhis odorata

Sweet cicely

attractive, feathery foliage • all parts of the plant can be used • sweet-smelling perennial • can be used as a diabetic sugar substitute

What is it?
Sweet cicely is a lacy, aromatic, multi-branched perennial plant with stout, hollow stems. It stands 1–1.5 m (3–5 ft) high and is nearly as broad as it is tall.

What to look for
The leaves are finely cut and frond-like, up to 50 cm (20 in) long and are a lighter green on their under surface. The oblong to ovate sections of leaf are lobed and have serrated edges. The flower stems terminate above the leaves in compound umbels of white flowers, which bloom between May and June. The seeds ripen between July and August.

Where to look
Look for sweet cicely on banks near running water, in grassy areas, as part of hedges and colonizing hilly or mountainous regions. It is also often found near human habitations. Although it requires moist, well-drained land in order to thrive, it tolerates a range of soil types, from light to heavy. A good place to seek out sweet-smelling cicely is on the edges of a woodland area, where the sunshine is more dappled.

As the seeds ripen they form a fibrous outer shell. For use in its raw state the seed is used when it is still green.

Forager's checklist

✔ **Leaves smell strongly of aniseed when crushed**

✔ **Can be found growing at the end of the winter season**

✔ **Large umbels of white flowers early in the year when little else is in bloom**

✔ **More likely to be found in mountainous areas**

✔ **Requires open or partial shade**

When to look for it

Cicely's young leaves are produced from late winter/early spring right through to early in the following winter. The seeds appear only after the flowering period (May–June) and after the little, green, cucumber-shaped fruits have ripened (July–August). Once the flowers develop the leaves lose much of their potency.

What does it taste like?

The overwhelming taste from all parts of the cicely plant is sweet aniseed. Some say that the seeds have the strongest, most intense flavour, while others prefer the leaves.

How is it used?

Cicely leaves can be eaten raw – try them chopped with yoghurt, whipped cream or sprinkled on top of a trifle. Cooked, they impart an excellent flavour to vegetables, and take away the sharp acidity of some types of stewed fruit. Dried cicely leaves make a wonderful food flavouring and are a component of bouquet garni. The dried leaves also make a tea substitute. The highly prized seeds have an intensity of flavour that works well in dishes where you might otherwise add anise or fennel. An oil is extracted from the seeds and used to flavour chartreuse. The root of the sweet cicely should be thoroughly cleaned and can then be eaten raw or cooked along with other vegetables to add flavour.

Large umbels of white flowers appear above fern-like foliage in later spring through to early summer.

Sweet Cicely

Petroselinum crispum

Parsley

used as a medicinal herb since the Middle Ages • shiny, bright-green leaves • a strong flavour means it is used sparingly • a rich source of vitamins and minerals

What is it?
This hairless biennial herb grows from a sturdy taproot with solid stems reaching about 70 cm (28 in) with a spread of about 35 cm (14 in).

What to look for
The leaves of the parsley plant are shiny and bright green: the lower ones are in triangular segments up to 2.5 cm (1 in) long with either scalloped or serrated edges; the upper ones are divided into three leaflets. The flat-topped umbels of yellowish flowers are compound, 2.5–5 cm (1–2 in) across and open from June to August; the seeds ripen July–September.

Where to look
This sturdy herb is likely to be found on sandy or rocky banks, on grassy waste ground and even coastal regions – anywhere that has moist, well-drained soil. It tolerates soils ranging from light (sandy) to heavy (clay), but requires at least partial sun – full sun is best. Its natural range is central and southern Europe, but parsley can be found naturalized in more northerly regions, including Britain.

When to look for it
Picking the leaves regularly stimulates the plant into producing fresh growth, so it is worth looking out for parsley right through its growing cycle. However, always leave sufficient leaf on the plant to sustain it if you want to benefit from seeds, which ripen in early autumn (around September), and make sure not to damage the flower stems.

What does it taste like?
The pungent, aromatic flavour of parsley, sometimes described as having nutty undertones, has a real presence and is therefore

The leaves of parsley are a bright, fresh-green colour with finely divided leaflets at the end of a long stem.

used mostly with moderation. The leaves are highly aromatic and because of the high levels of chlorophyll they contain, make a useful breath freshener.

How is it used?

Parsley is an excellent source of vitamins A, B and, especially, C, as well as being rich in magnesium, iron and calcium. The leaves can be eaten raw as a garnish or used as a salad ingredient, adding a real depth of flavour to the mix. The leaves can also be cooked – the Japanese deep-fry them in a light tempura. The leaves of parsley are easier to freeze than dry, but dried parsley makes an excellent food flavouring and is an ingredient in bouquet garni as well as being a tea substitute (fresh leaves can also be used).

Try it in

Parsley and Herb Salad (see page 220).

Forager's checklist

✔ **Highly aromatic leaves**
✔ **Plant has a rounded shape with curly leaves**
✔ **Clump-forming in habit**
✔ **Favours growing in limestone regions**
✔ **Fruits are about 2.5 mm (⅛ in) long and broadly egg-shaped.**

Parsley

Parsley sends up compound umbels of small yellowish flowers in its second summer of growth.

Phragmites australis

Reed

vigorous, invasive reed grass • long connected to human
populations worldwide • contains a sugar-rich sap • all parts
can be used

What is it?
A quick-growing perennial reed grass with a
rhizomatous root system. This grass reaches
about 3.5 m (11 ft) when in flower and will
spread to take up any available space.

What to look for
The flat, linear, sword-like leaves are 1–2.5 cm
(½–1 in) wide and about 65 cm (25 in) long.
Grey-green leaves take on more russet shades in
the autumn. In late summer, the plant throws up
tall, bamboo-like spikes terminating in brownish,
silky, plume-like flowers, followed by grain-like
seed heads.

Where to look
A water-loving plant, reed grass's natural
habitats include marshes, bogs, lakesides and
the quiet edges of streams and rivers. It will not
tolerate dry soil nor very acid soil, but it will
thrive in full sun and partial shade. It seems to
prefer disturbed ground, such as that churned
up by dredging, and is found throughout Europe
and in temperate regions in both hemispheres.

When to look for it
So much of the plant is edible and at so many
stages of its growth cycle that you can usefully
seek it from early spring when the new shoots
first start to appear, to late autumn when the
seed has fully ripened.

What does it taste like?
You receive no easy clues to the sweet sugary
flavour of the reed, which some people liken to
liquorice, as the leaves don't have the aromatic
fragrance of many other food-rich wild plants.

Plumes of grain-like seed heads break
from sheaths at the top of stalks that
stand proud of the surrounding foliage.

The reed is a vigorous, invasive plant, popularly eaten throughout the world due to its high sugar content.

Forager's checklist

✔ **Most at home in open areas of wetland**

✔ **Very tall grass rapidly forming impenetrable beds**

✔ **Plume-like flowers are dark brown to purple**

✔ **Needs still or slow-moving water in which to establish itself**

✔ **Leaves taper, narrowing to a slender point**

How is it used?

Young roots can be dried and ground to make a porridge or boiled like potatoes. You can also boil and eat the underground stems, though you may find them a little tough. Better eating are the newly emerged stems. Leave the stems to develop (but before they flower) and grind them down into flour. Grind young leaves down into a powder, mix it with wheat flour and you have the basis of Japanese-style dumplings. The seeds are nutritious, whether raw or boiled. And if you have a sweet tooth, collect the gum oozing from a wounded stem, roll into a ball and simply eat it as a sweet, or leave it near an open fire to brown and become more toffee-like.

Rorippa nasturtium-aquaticum

Watercress

grows in great profusion • high vitamin C content • can be harvested throughout the year • pungent aroma

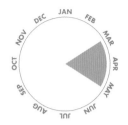

What is it?
A mound-forming aquatic perennial with a floating or creeping habit. This plant can become invasive. Individual plants can reach about 50 cm (20 in) and a spread of about 1 m (3 ft), though for all practical purposes its spread is indefinite.

What to look for
The leaf of watercress is a deep, rich green colour, divided into opposite-growing lobes. The lateral lobes are often ovate (egg-shaped), sometimes rectangular, and the terminal lobe distinctly cordate (heart-shaped). Leaves are borne on jointed, hollow stems. The small, white flowers, which bloom in terminal clusters from May to September, are about 5 mm (¼ in) across. The seeds that follow ripen between July and September.

Where to look
Adjacent to or standing in ponds, bogs, fens, the edges of streams and drainage ditches, anywhere, where there is running water is the place to seek out watercress. It will not grow in full shade, but does tolerate partial shade – its preference is for full sun. This is a lowland plant and is native throughout Europe.

When to look for it
This plant grows so abundantly you can enjoy its crop of leaves right through its active growing season (March–September), but young leaves have less flavour than the older ones. Its leaves stay green in autumn. Its main season is probably spring (March–May), when watercress is valued as a tonic.

What does it taste like?
The leaves of watercress have a strong, hot, peppery flavour. You can also collect the ripe seeds in autumn and grind these down to make a pungent mustard.

How is it used?
Although you can eat watercress leaves raw, it is probably better to cook foraged leaves unless

The hotness of watercress leaves makes them an interesting addition to more traditional salad ingredients.

they come from clean, fast-flowing water (see Caution below). If you are looking to add a little zing to the salad bowl, the peppery hotness of watercress fits the bill perfectly. These leaves have so much flavour you can easily turn them into delicious full-bodied soups. Start off with a good-quality stock, add the watercress leaves and any bulkier items – potatoes or root vegetables – according to taste.

Try it in
Watercress Soup (see page 221).

Caution
Because watercress can be host to liver fluke parasites, never use raw leaves growing in water that could be contaminated by animal waste. Boiling the leaves destroys this parasite. Always wash any watercress leaves thoroughly, no matter what their source, to remove snail or insect infestation.

Watercress amply demonstrates the vigorous growth patterns that are associated with water-loving plants.

Forager's checklist

- ✔ Usually found in chalk or limestone regions
- ✔ Seed pods short and ovoid seeds are arranged inside in two rows
- ✔ Leaves are alternate (lobes opposite)
- ✔ Flowers arranged in racemes (elongated flower clusters)
- ✔ Never use raw leaves from plants growing in muddy or stagnant water

Watercress

Smyrnium olusatrum

Alexanders, horse parsley

can be used raw or cooked • widely distributed • erect, glabrous
biennial • leaves arranged in groups of three

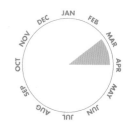

What is it?
A bushy, erect, solid-stemmed biennial herb that
was introduced into Britain by the Romans some
2,000 years ago and remained popular until
around 200 years ago. It grows to about 1.2 m
(4 ft) and has a spread of 75 cm (30 in).

What to look for
The tuberous taproot of *Smyrnium olusatrum* is
fragile and fleshy, while the shiny, dark-green
leaves are arranged three on a stalk, attached
to the stem by a prominent sheath, and are
slightly serrated. The upper leaves are opposite.
The flowers are yellow-green, opening in
compound umbels April–June, and its seeds
ripen June–August.

Where to look
This plant prefers neglected waste areas and
scrub, sometimes woodland margins, where it
receives little interference. It will tolerate light
shade and full sun. It often favours coastal
regions, such as sea cliffs and ditches, and
prefers a moist, well-drained soil. Native to the
Mediterranean region, it is now naturalized
throughout much of Europe.

When to look for it
The stems of this herb are perhaps at their best
for foraging just before the flowers open, so
keep a sharp lookout in March and early April.
Another season of interest for the forager is
winter (November–February). Alexanders comes
into leaf in the autumn, providing a tasty salad
ingredient at a time when home-grown choice is
often extremely limited.

What does it taste like?
The taste Alexanders is most often likened to is
that of celery, though perhaps more bitter and

Flowers have both male and female
reproductive organs and plants are
self-fertile.

Forager's checklist

✔ **Has a pungent smell when crushed**

✔ **Apart from the seeds, all parts have a celery-like flavour**

✔ **Ripe fruits are black**

✔ **Can be found growing in damp sand**

✔ **Roots become more tender if kept cool during the winter**

pungent. Indeed, this herb fell out of favour largely because of the introduction of celery. The seeds are aromatic and spicy.

How is it used?

Treat the stems, cut low down just before the flowers open, as you would asparagus – boiled until just tender and served with butter and pepper. You can use the leaves and young shoots raw in salads or add them to your soup and stew ingredients. But omit the celery, as the flavour is very similar. You can also chop the flower heads and throw them into the salad bowl to add an extra taste to the mix. The flower heads left on the plant yield useful seeds – aromatic and spicy. Ground up, use them instead of pepper. The fleshy roots (best in the plant's first year) can be boiled as a soup ingredient like celery or try them as an alternative to parsnips.

For the best flavour cut the stems close to the ground and cook gently until just tender.

Symphytum officinale

Comfrey, knitbone

dark-green, hairy leaves • invasive perennial • widely distributed
• requires good drainage, but constantly moist soil

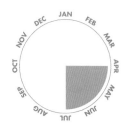

What is it?

An upright, bushy perennial herb with leaves and stems covered with short, bristly hairs. It reaches 50 cm–1.2 m (20 in–4ft) and has a spread of about half its height.

What to look for

Comfrey leaves are very distinctive – broadly lanceolate (lance-shaped), dark green, covered in stiff hairs on their under surface, and markedly reticulated. Stem leaves are alternate and 15–30 cm (6–12 in) long. Nodding clusters of bell-shaped yellowy-white, pink or purple flowers open between late spring and early autumn (May–October).

Can be mistaken for

When comfrey is not in flower, it is possible to mistake it for a foxglove (*Digitalis* spp.).

Where to look

This perennial herb is a sun-loving plant, although it will tolerate moderate shade. Look on open ground or woodland fringes, where the canopy is light and broken. It does not appreciate the ground drying out between drinks. Streamside banks and drainage ditches are, therefore, good sites. Given these

conditions, comfrey can grow vigorously and become invasive, spreading principally by self-sown seed. It has become established through much of Europe.

When to look for it

Because of some health concerns regarding the use of older comfrey leaves (see Caution below), it is best to use the new spring and early summer growth of leaves and stalks (April–June/July).

What does it taste like?

It must be said that comfrey is not to everybody's taste. Many are put off by its hairiness and its mucilaginous (glue-like) texture. Older leaves are quite bitter-tasting.

The rather glue-like quality of raw comfrey leaves is not going to appeal to all palates.

How is it used?

Known for centuries as a medicinal herb, its name 'comfrey' comes from the Latin *confervere*, meaning to 'grow together'; it was used in medieval times to help broken bones mend, giving rise to one of its common names, 'knitbone'. Today, young comfrey leaves are more likely to be used as a salad ingredient (very finely chopped to minimize the presence of its hairs), or lightly boiled and used as you would spinach (the hairiness tends to lessen when cooked). You can also use young comfrey shoots (blanched is best) as a replacement for asparagus. In addition, try using the cleaned, peeled and chopped roots as a soup ingredient, or roast and grind them down for use as a coffee substitute.

Try it in

Comfrey Fritters (see page 222).

Caution

Comfrey contains small amounts of a toxic alkaloid and is best avoided by people with any form of liver disorder. There is almost none of this substance in the young leaves, however, but concentrations are higher in the shoots and roots.

Forager's checklist

✔ Grows well in heavy soils (clay)

✔ Brownish-black fruits about 4 mm (⅙ in) long follow on from the flowers

✔ New plants will regenerate from the smallest fragment of root left in the ground

✔ Deeply buried, sturdy taproot

✔ New leaves and young stems to be used

Comfrey

Clusters of bell-shaped flowers open over a long period. Typical colours are pink, mauve or creamy white.

Typha latifolia

Cattail, bulrush, reed mace

vigorous waterside perennial • versatile food plant • widely
distributed • grows in wet soil or in standing water

Riverside Plants

What is it?

Grass-like, perennial, rhizomatous plant with
long, simple sword-like leaves and a sturdy dark-
brown flower spike topping a robust stem
reaching 3 m (10 ft) high. These plants are
invasive and have an indefinite spread.

What to look for

The leaves are 1–3 m (3–10 ft) long, grey-green
and sprout in groups of 12–16 from growing
points on the rhizome. The robust, upright stalk
is usually sufficiently tall that the flower spike it
bears is higher than the leaves. Flowers are tiny,
but produced in great profusion on a heavy
spadix. Flowers open in late spring through to
summer (May/June–August).

Where to look

This aquatic plant must have its feet in perpetually
wet soil or even in shallow standing water. The
ideal place to look is by streams, drainage
ditches, irrigation channels, estuaries, marshes,
fens, lakes and ponds. Although it prefers fresh
water, it will tolerate slightly brackish water.
Cattail will not tolerate shade and needs full sun.
It is a tolerant plant and has established itself
throughout Europe and most of the world.

The seeds of cattail can be roasted to
produce a pleasant, nutty flavour, or
ground down and added to flour.

When to look for it

You can harvest the rhizomes, which can be 60 cm (24 in) or more long, in late autumn through to early spring. This is when they are richest in starch (up to 40 per cent plus). Collect the young growing shoots in early spring (March–April) and the flower spikes when they are mature and full of pollen (around August–September).

What does it taste like?

This wonderful plant produces a range of interesting flavours to tempt the palate. The new shoots are reported to have a cucumber flavour, while the immature flower spike is likened to sweet corn. The seeds can also be used and roasting them brings out their nutty flavour.

How is it used?

Treat the central core of the starch-rich rhizome as you would a potato, or grind it down to a flour for mixing with wheat flour, or boil it down to form a syrup. The young spring shoots, up to about 50 cm (20 in) in length, are edible either raw, or cooked as a vegetable or added to your other soup ingredients. The immature flower spike is another useful soup ingredient and the protein-rich pollen from the mature flower spikes can be added to flour. It is good added to pancake batter. The seeds can be used raw or roasted and ground down into a flour – but they are small and you need to question whether the amount of time and energy this takes is really justified.

Forager's checklist

- ✔ Cannot grow in water deeper than about 75 cm (30 in)
- ✔ Leaves are thick and ribbon-like
- ✔ Brown flowers look golden yellow when they are full of pollen
- ✔ Leaves have parallel veining

Cattail

The still margins of large bodies of water make perfect breeding grounds for this vigorous perennial plant.

GRASSLAND PLANTS

You don't have to travel long distances to find the right type of 'grassland' able to support a good variety of green comestibles. Plants are adaptable, so inspect the culinary possibilities offered by neighbourhood vacant building sites, heaths, local parks and woods and abandoned gardens. And if you are in foraging range of meadows, fields, pastures and fens, then all the better. Where land is under cultivation, look in the field margins, those strips and corners and broken areas where nature is allowed to flourish because the space is too awkward to provide easy access for a tractor.

Aegopodium podagraria

Ground elder, goutweed

vigorous, invasive perennial weed • young growth has the best
flavour • thrives in shady places

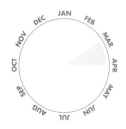

Grassland Plants

What is it?
Forming large mats of groundcover, this invasive
perennial weed spreads by an underground
network of slender rhizomes and rarely reaches
more than 1 m (3 ft) high. As many gardeners
will know, with some despair, ground elder is
very difficult to dislodge.

What to look for
The shiny mid- to dark-green leaves of ground
elder are 10–20 cm (4–8 in) long, deltate
(broadly triangular) and divided into ovate
segments. The leaf edges are irregularly
toothed. White flowers appear in compound
umbels borne on creeping hollow stems that
grow about 60 cm (2 ft) high between May
and August.

Where to look
Ground elder is an adaptable plant, able to
take advantage of a wide range of habitats.
These include grassland, forest edges,
hedgerows, abandoned gardens and waste and
disturbed ground. It will also grow in a range of
conditions from deep or dappled shade to full
sun. It does not, however, like the ground to dry
out between watering. Ground elder is thought
to have been introduced into Britain by the
Romans, as a culinary herb and a medicinal
plant, and has been distributed throughout
Europe as an escapee from the gardens of
religious orders.

When to look for it
The leaves and stems have the best flavour if
you get to them in the spring, before the flowers
have formed. Try picking the shoots when they
are no more than 15 cm (6 in) high in
March–April.

The strongly flavoured leaves of ground
elder are arranged in groups of three
and are best picked young.

Forager's checklist

✔ **Stems are hollow and grooved**

✔ **Plant stands stout and erect**

✔ **Outer flower petals are larger than the inner ones**

✔ **Particularly favours disturbed ground**

✔ **Stems rarely taller than 1 m (3 ft)**

✔ **Veins of the leaves feel slightly rough to the touch**

Ground Elder

What does it taste like?

It is reported to have a distinctive tangy, pungent flavour, which is not universally popular. The stems are said to have a strong scent of fennel. It is still popularly eaten as a vegetable in Scandinavia and Russia.

How is it used?

The young leaves and stems can be used raw as a salad ingredient or included in soups to add an unusual, tangy flavour. The leaves and stems can also be treated much as you would spinach – cook them in a tiny amount of water and a generous knob of butter. Stir them constantly until they are just tender. Season to taste and add more butter if necessary at the end.

Used for both food and medicine in the Middle Ages, ground elder is now regarded as an invasive weed.

Agaricus campestris

Field mushroom

edible grassland species • young cap is strongly convex • short
stem • can be found in large numbers after wet weather

Grassland Plants

What is it?
A short-stemmed white mushroom, closely
related to the familiar cultivated button
mushroom (*Agaricus bisporus*) that is widely
available in shops. The cap is 2.5–11 cm
(1–4½ in) across. The stem is 2.5–6 cm (1–2½
in) long and up to 2.5 cm (1 in) thick, tapering
slightly towards the base.

What to look for
The cap is strongly convex at first, becoming
flatter with age, and it varies from white, smooth
and shiny (when young) to brown, fibrous and
scaly (when mature). The gills under the cap
are pinkish at first, turning dark brown with age.
The stem often has a simple white ring. The
flesh of the cap is soft and white and does not
discolour when cut; the stem turns slightly pink
when cut.

Can be mistaken for
This popular forager's mushroom can be
mistaken for the yellow-staining mushroom
(*Agaricus xanthodermus*). This poisonous fungus
causes sickness and diarrhoea, but is not
deadly. The first thing you should notice when
collecting is an unpleasant inky odour. Alerted
by this, the cap is flatter than that of the field

mushroom, the stem ring is more prominent and
the base of the stem turns yellow when cut.

Where to look
This common European mushroom favours
grassland, meadows, fields, lawns and pastures.
You may be well rewarded by mounting a
collecting expedition a day or so after rain,
concentrating your endeavours in fields grazed
by horses, cows and sheep. Although mostly
associated with open ground, you will also find
field mushrooms in grassy areas among
woodland trees.

The gills, found under the cap of
a young field mushroom, are pinkish
in colour.

When to look for it

This is principally an autumn mushroom (September–November), though early summer (June) can also be rewarding. Much depends on the rainfall, so keep a sharp eye out any time from early summer onwards.

What does it taste like?

This is the most commonly eaten wild mushroom in the UK and has a pleasant odour and taste. It has a stronger presence than cultivated species and some people report that it has a faint taste of anise.

How is it used?

As long as your specimens are free from insect infestation, field mushrooms can be eaten raw and in salads. There is no need to peel them, just give them a wipe over with a cloth. Cut away and discard the base of the stem. For maximum flavour, cut the mushroom into good-sized slices and fry them in butter, seasoned to taste. Use a high heat and cook only for a few minutes – otherwise too much water will be released and the result will be rubbery.

Try it in

Wild Mushroom Ring Mould (see page 224).

Caution

If the flesh of the cap turns red when bruised, discard it – you may have picked a mushroom that is a poisonous lookalike.

This mushroom species favours open grassland and can be found in abundance a day or two after rain.

Forager's checklist

✔ **Old mushrooms prone to insect infestation**
✔ **Found in groups, sometimes forming 'fairy rings'**
✔ **Stem ring not likely to survive until maturity**
✔ **Gills enclosed in a white veil when young**

Field Mushroom

Cichorium intybus

Chicory

tough perennial plant • attractive, daisy-like flowers • can be used raw or cooked • has a white, milky sap

What is it?
A rather sprawling perennial herb with stiffly erect stems and a long taproot. It reaches 50–150 cm (20 in–5 ft) high, with a spread of 30–50 cm (12–20 in).

What to look for
The most distinguishing feature is its pale-blue, daisy-like flowers, which open and close each day, but remain open only when the weather is cooler. Chicory can be found in bloom between July and October. The alternate leaves are basal, spirally arranged and resemble those of a dandelion. The stems are grooved, branched and vary from smooth to hairy. The plant grows from a very long, sturdy taproot.

Where to look
This grassland plant can often be found in fields and meadows from Scandinavia in the North right down to the top of Africa in the South. In many countries it is also the driver's companion, being one of the few plants of any height whose roots are robust enough to break through the compacted earth commonly associated with roadside edges. It particularly favours moist, well-drained chalky soil.

The plant is self-fertile and is pollinated principally by bees. It is a good plant for attracting wildlife.

When to look for it
Look for chicory leaves in late spring and early summer (May–June) before the flowers develop as they have a better flavour. The flowers are also edible, and you can pick these any time between July and October.

What does it taste like?
Chicory has a pleasant, slightly bitter flavour. The bitterness in the leaves increases when the plant is in flower. The flowers, also edible, have the same bitter flavour. Once roasted, the taproot's bitter flavour is overlayered with hints of caramel.

How is it used?
Chicory leaves can be eaten raw or cooked as a vegetable, though choose early summer leaves in raw salads to minimize the rather bitter taste. With older leaves, it is best to boil them in a few changes of water. The wonderful sky-blue colour of the edible flowers makes a wonderful addition to a salad bowl. The deep-growing root of chicory probably has the most devotees. You can treat it like other root vegetables, such as parsnip, and roast it, or boil it and use it as a food flavouring for soups and gravies. One-year-old roots have a milder flavour; those more than two years old can be quite bitter. Chicory roots are also ground down after roasting to make a caffeine-free coffee substitute.

Try it in
Pear, Chicory and Gorgonzola Bruschetta (see page 226).

Blanched leaves have a better flavour than unblanched ones, while winter-picked leaves tend to have a milder taste.

Forager's checklist

- ✔ Found in an open sunny position
- ✔ Seeds ripen between August and October
- ✔ Requires moist, well-drained soil
- ✔ Stems support only a few leaves
- ✔ Flower heads are up to 4.5 cm (1¾ in) across

Chicory

Filipendula ulmaria

Meadowsweet

regarded by the Druids as a sacred plant • erect, perennial herb •
used to flavour food and alcohol • sweetly scented

Grassland Plants

What is it?
An erect, herbaceous perennial herb 1–1.8 m
(3–6 ft) high, with a spread of about 30–90 cm
(12–36 in).

What to look for
The leaves are dark green on their upper
surfaces, while their undersides are silvery and
covered in fine hairs. Leaves are divided into
pairs of leaflets of varying size, up to about
7 cm (3 in) long, and have serrated edges. The
erect stems of meadowsweet are grooved and
reddish, sometimes verging on purple. The
creamy white to yellowish-white flowers are
sweetly fragrant and bloom in dense panicles
(branched clusters) from June to September.

Where to look
This plant does not like to dry out, so you need
to look for it in wet grassland that is favoured
with a constant supply of water, bogs, wet
woodland and fens. It is tolerant of a wide
range of soils, from neutral to alkaline, and will
grow in heavy clay soils and light sandy
ground. Both dappled shade and full sun (if the
water supply is reliable) will suit. It is found
throughout most of Europe.

When to look for it
The leaves (especially the young ones) and
the flowers are the most desirable parts of
meadowsweet, so spring and early summer
(April–June) is when you will find maximum
new leaf growth. Then from June to September
the flowers are available for foraging.

What does it taste like?
The flowers of meadowsweet have a heady
sweetness (both in aroma and flavour) that
some people report as being overpowering,
even sickly. The leaves are also sweet, but
they have an entirely different flavour from that
of the flowers.

The distinctive leaves of meadowsweet
are divided into 2–5 pairs of leaflets
that vary greatly in size.

How is it used?

All parts of meadowsweet are worth the forager's attention. The fresh new leaves, flower heads and roots can all be made into a tasty tea substitute, while the young leaves make a flavoursome addition to soups and sauces. Once dried, you can use the leaves as a sweetener and food flavouring. For a slightly different taste, use the flower heads as a sweetener when cooking some of the more tart-tasting fruits, such as gooseberries or rhubarb – try 8–9 flower heads to 1 kg (2 lb) of fruit. The flower heads have traditionally been added to alcohol, such as beer, wine and mead. Indeed, the name 'meadowsweet' is probably a corruption of 'meadwort' rather than an indication that the plant ever particularly favoured meadows.

Forager's checklist

- ✔ Leaves are aromatic, slightly astringent, when rubbed between your fingers
- ✔ Seeds ripen between September and October
- ✔ Flowers held on erect stems well above the foliage
- ✔ It is never found in acid peat conditions
- ✔ An attractive plant for wildlife

The flowers, along with the leaves and roots, can be made into tea. They can also be added to beer or wine.

Meadowsweet

Langermannia gigantea (syn. *Calvatia gigantea*)

Giant puffball

one of the tastiest fungus species • no visible stem • spores borne
internally • can be found singly or in groups

Grassland Plants

What is it?
This is a potentially very large, approximately round fungus of exceptionally fine taste. It has no visible stem and seems to have magically popped out of the ground. When fully grown (though not then best for eating), giant puffballs have been recorded as weighing 25 kg (55 lb), and have measured 1.5 m (5 ft) across, while standing more than 25 cm (10 in) high.

What to look for
Size and shape are the two unmistakable features of this fungus, though smaller, immature specimens make the best eating. Shape is variable – sometimes regular, like a soccer ball, other times more irregular and blob-like. Specimens measuring 10–30 cm (4–12 in) across is what you should expect to see, with a white, leathery, smooth outer skin. The puffball's flesh is also white – if it is yellow or darkened to a pale brown and is full of tiny air pockets, it is too old for eating. The whiter and denser the flesh, the better the flavour.

Where to look
The giant puffball is found in grassy areas, in fields, meadows, pastures, gardens and woodland throughout Europe. It prefers a rich soil that has been improved by the addition of composted organic material.

When to look for it
For such a large fungus it develops remarkably quickly – the fruiting body can develop within just a couple of weeks and then soon starts to rot away, having reached maturity and released its spores. The peak time for the giant puffball is around mid-summer (July), though any time between late spring and early autumn (May–September) is possible.

Often found in association with nettles in grassy areas, the giant puffball is a spectacular find.

Forager's checklist

✔ There are no external gills and the stem is not visible

✔ Found in deciduous woods thriving on decomposing leaf litter

✔ Because of local atmospheric pollution, it is best not to take specimens from roadsides

✔ Can reach full size in as little as a week

✔ The denser and whiter the flesh, the better tasting it is likely to be

Found either in groups or individually, it is unlikely you could mistake the smooth, rounded shape for anything else.

What does it taste like?

Some people claim that the flesh is reminiscent of tofu, but most agree that young specimens have an intense and exquisite 'mushroomy' flavour. Older, more porous, specimens tend to take on the flavour of whatever accompanied them in cooking.

How is it used?

All parts of the giant puffball are edible – you do not have to peel it. Although not prone to insect infestation like many other fungi species, you may find the outer skin has been breached by insects in isolated areas. Just shake out any unwanted interlopers. With puffballs, size is not the most important thing – small specimens can be sliced into steaks, coated in seasoned crumbs and fried in butter. Try them prepared this way with a few slices of bacon. Even an immature puffball could yield several kilos of flesh – more than can reasonably be eaten at one sitting. If you find yourself in this situation, slice and lightly fry the flesh and then freeze it. You will lose the wonderful texture of the fresh fungi, but at least it will not go to waste.

Try it in

Braised Chinese Puffballs (see page 227).

Lathyrus montanus

Bitter vetch

attractive reddish-purple flowers • seeds can be eaten in
moderation • upright herbaceous perennial herb • used as
a vegetable since the Middle Ages

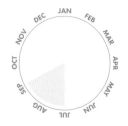

What is it?
This member of the pea family is a tufted
herbaceous perennial. It grows 50–60 cm
(20–24 in) high and has a spread of about
30–60 cm (12–24 in).

What to look for
The leaves are alternate and an eye-catching
blue-green, divided into pairs of leaflets
approximately oval in shape and about 5 cm
(2 in) long. The racemes of flowers, which open
in spring through to early summer (April–July),
are reddish-purple and about 1.5 cm (¾ in)
long. The flowers are followed by reddish-brown
seed pods 2.5–4.5 cm (1–1¾ in) long.

Where to look
This is a plant of sunny banks and grassland or
the light, dappled shade found on the margins
of woodland. It requires moist, well-drained soil
that is neutral to acid and will tolerate light,
sandy ground as well as heavy clay. Bitter vetch
is found throughout temperate Europe.

When to look for it
The seeds of bitter vetch, which you should not
eat to excess (see Caution below), ripen
between July and September, after the flowers

have gone over. The roots can be taken at any
time, but are best taken from young plants.

What does it taste like?
Once the root nodules have been processed
they take on the flavour of liquorice. The seeds
have been likened to the taste of sweet chestnuts
(see pages 30–31)

Starting out reddish-purple in spring,
the flowers of bitter vetch fade to blue
as they age during the summer.

Grassland Plants

How is it used?

In use since the Middle Ages, the edible tubers of bitter vetch are first dried and then used as a flavouring for food and drinks (even for whisky in Scotland). This material was formerly used as a health-giving tonic to stave off the pangs of hunger. The seed is cooked and used as a vegetable in much the same way as you would use sweet chestnuts.

Try it in

Hot Vetch and Chicken Salad (see page 228).

Caution

If ingested in very large quantities – making up to 30 per cent of your diet, it has been estimated – the seeds of bitter vetch (and many other *Lathyrus* species) can cause a serious disease known as lathyrism, which affects the nervous system. Eaten in normal quantities, however, these seeds should not represent a health concern.

Forager's checklist

✔ **Not normally found on chalky soil**

✔ **Flowers have both male and female organs**

✔ **Upright stems**

✔ **Can be found in great numbers where the ground is healthy**

Bitter vetch is a native of grassland, mixed pastures and open woodland and enjoys moist, well-drained soil.

Lepiota procera

Parasol mushroom

white flesh that does not change colour • brown scales develop as fungus grows • distinctive ring on stem • grows singly or in small groups

Grassland Plants

What is it?
This prized edible fungus has a pronounced egg-shaped cap when immature, but this flattens out as it ages, though there is always a small umbo (prominence) in the centre. The cap can measure 10–25 cm (4–10 in) across and it stands 15–30 cm (6–12 in) high, with a non-bulbous stem up to 2.5 cm (1 in) wide at the base.

What to look for
The parasol mushroom's outer skin is brown, but this breaks up to produce a scaly appearance

The excellent flavour of this grassland species makes it a firm favourite with wild-food foragers.

as the fungus grows and expands. The flesh you can see between the scales is initially white, turning darker with age. The umbo, however, remains its original brown colour throughout. The stem has the same colouration as the cap – brown turning scaly with age. The soft flesh is white and does not change colour when cut or bruised. Under the cap, the crowded, white-coloured gills sometimes turn reddish or tan as the fungus ages.

Can be mistaken for
The parasol mushroom can be mistaken for the shaggy parasol (*Lepiota rhacodes*). This fungus prefers a shadier growing site than *L. procera*, but it can more readily be differentiated by its flesh, which turns reddish when cut. The shaggy parasol can cause stomach upsets if eaten and some people experience a skin allergy after handling it.

Where to look
You will sometimes find parasol mushrooms in light woodland or at the margins of woodland, but it is more commonly found in grassland, woodland clearings and in open ground near paths and roadside verges throughout Europe.

When to look for it

After rainy weather in the warm months from mid-summer through to autumn (August–October) is the best time to hunt for this fungus. The best time to pick the parasol mushroom is just as the cap starts to open out – you may sacrifice something in size, but the extra flavour more than compensates.

What does it taste like?

The flesh of the parasol mushroom is quite delicious – sweet and nutty – and the smell is fresh and earthy.

How is it used?

While the flesh of the cap is prized by fungus aficionados, the stem is woody and should be discarded. The gills are not attached to the stem, so it should part company very readily. If you have a not-too-large specimen, cook the cap whole, protected in batter or breadcrumbs to stop the flesh soaking up too much fat or oil. If the cap is still domed and egg-shaped, fill it up with chopped bacon and caramelized onions and bake in the oven until brown. The parasol mushroom can be kept in the refrigerator for a day or two before cooking and once sliced it dries well for later use.

Try it in

Parasol Platters (see page 229).

Forager's checklist

- ✔ Gills are not attached to the stem
- ✔ Double-edged ring becomes detached and can be moved up and down the stem
- ✔ Stem flesh does not change colour when rubbed or bruised
- ✔ Stem is slender, not bulbous
- ✔ Can often be found growing on disturbed ground

Parasol Mushroom

The long stem of the parasol mushroom, standing as high as 30 cm (12 in), makes it easy to spot.

Lepista saeva

Field blewit, blue-leg

distinctive coloured stem • available late in the year • irregular-shaped caps • fruiting bodies often found in rings

Grassland Plants

What is it?
A medium-sized, ground-growing fungus with a usually convex, sometimes irregular leaf-shaped cap, 3.5–10 cm (1½–4 in) high. The cap is 5–12 cm (2–5 in) across and the stem 1.5–2.5 cm (¾–1 in) wide at its sometimes swollen base.

What to look for
The obvious feature of the field blewit is its distinctive lilac-streaked stem, which is short and stout and has no ring. The cap, which can be flattened or even depressed, is pale to mid-brown, smooth and non-sticky, with wavy margins. The flesh is white, thick and firm. The gills underneath the cap are densely arranged and have whitish to pinky flesh.

Can be mistaken for
Where the shade from trees (especially beech) is heavier, you may mistake the tasty wood blewit (*Lepista nuda*) for the field blewit. Although very alike, the woodland species has lilac-coloured gills. Watch out, however, for the poisonous livid entoloma (*Entoloma lividum*), which causes acute gastric problems. This fungus is most readily distinguished by the lack of lilac colouring on its stem and the yellow gills of young specimens.

The flesh of the cap is white and firm to the touch. Margins are incurved when young, becoming wavy later.

Forager's checklist

✔ **Often appear in the same spot more than once**

✔ **Sometimes found singly, but more usually in groups or rings**

✔ **Gills are easy to separate from the flesh**

✔ **Smell strongly aromatic**

✔ **Flesh is firm; dries and freezes well**

The base of the stem is often swollen, there is no ring and there is distinctive lilac streaking.

Where to look

Grassy pastures and the margins of woodlands throughout Europe are likely places to find the field blewit. And if you are fortunate, you may even find them popping up in your lawn at home. Keep your eyes peeled for them on waste ground, near roadside verges and on open ground beside paths and tracks.

When to look for it

This is an autumn to early-winter fungus (September to November), though you may be lucky and find some in mild years well into December. It is worth looking any time in December until the first frosts arrive and see them off.

What does it taste like?

This fungus tastes and smells strongly aromatic, almost perfumed – not at all 'mushroomy', as you might expect. Some people report them having a pleasant nutty flavour.

How is it used?

There is no wastage with this fungus, so wipe your specimen to make sure it is clean, then remove and finely chop the fleshy stem. Pack this around the cap with onions, season to taste and cook in bacon fat. If you don't want to fry them, they are also tasty stewed, though eating them raw is not recommended since some people experience stomach upsets this way. Any extra mushrooms can be frozen or dried for later use.

Try it in

Blewit Baskets (see page 230).

Common mallow

variable in form • widely distributed perennial • long flowering
period • can be eaten raw or cooked • long used as a food plant

What is it?
Depending on region, common mallow can be
an annual, biennial or perennial. It is known
to have been used in ancient Greece and Rome,
as well as in Egypt and China. It grows to
1.5 m (5 ft), sometimes more, and has a spread
of about 60 cm (24 in).

What to look for
This very variable species can be lax or upright,
single- or multi-stemmed, slender or robust, hairy
or (occasionally) non-hairy, but usually clump-
forming. The leaves are crinkly – basal leaves
nearly disc-shaped and shallowly lobed; those
on the stem, deeply lobed. The five-petalled
flowers are purplish-pink and its extended
flowering season is between June and October.

Where to look
Originating in southern Europe, common mallow
can now be found naturalized throughout the
temperate zones of the Continent. Fields,
pastures, the grassy margins of woods, roadside
verges, waste ground and the protected areas
near the coast are all likely habitats for this
herb. Its preference is for full sun, but it will
tolerate light shade. It requires moist, well-
drained soil in order to thrive.

When to look for it
The best time to pick the leaves is in the summer
when they are still pale-coloured. Wash them
well, discarding any that show evidence of
having been used by insects for their egg-laying
activities. The unripe seed is worth collecting in
August and September for its flavour, though
they are small and patience is required.

What does it taste like?
The tiny round seeds, known as 'cheeses', have
a pleasant nutty flavour, while the leaves,
though pleasant-tasting, do have rather a
gelatinous, gluey consistency.

The young seeds can be eaten raw as
a snack and the fully ripe seeds also
have a good flavour.

As well as being an attractive purplish-pink colour, mallow flowers make a tasty addition to the salad bowl.

Forager's checklist

✔ **Flowers up to 5 cm (2 in) across**

✔ **Basal leaves up to 10 cm (4 in) in diameter**

✔ **Pink flowers are marked with purple veining**

✔ **Leaves remain green throughout the growing year**

How is it used?

Used raw, you can add young common mallow leaves to the salad bowl instead of the familiar lettuce. The flowers, too, have a mild flavour and can be added to your salad ingredients to give an extra splash of colour. The leaves make a good thickening agent in soups or you can deep-fry them until they are crisp. The unripe seed is fine to eat just as a tasty snack food. Dry the leaves and you have a pleasant-tasting tea substitute. Not to everybody's taste because of their gluey consistency, you can cook the leaves in a little boiling water and treat them as a vegetable.

Origanum vulgare

Common oregano

aromatic perennial herb • mound-like or upright habit • can be
used dried or fresh • used to flavour food for over 2,000 years

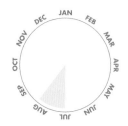

Grassland Plants

What is it?

The botanical and common names for this plant cause a good measure of confusion, as common oregano (*O. vulgare*) is also known as wild marjoram. Common oregano is a bushy semi-woody aromatic perennial herb, growing 75–100 cm (30–36 in) high.

What to look for

The leaves of this herb are opposite, ovate and untoothed, growing up to about 5 cm (2 in) long. The tiny, purple-pink, tubular flowers – about 3–4 mm (⅛ in) long – bloom throughout the summer and autumn between July and October in terminal panicles.

Where to look

The type of dry, well-drained grassy areas you might encounter on hedge banks, for example, or in meadows and fields is where you need to look for common oregano. Too much moisture will cause the roots to rot. For the best flavour, pick from plants that are fully open to the sun. This native of the Mediterranean is now naturalized throughout most of Europe.

The leaves of common oregano are distinctly egg-shaped (ovate), with the broader end at the base.

Forager's checklist

✔ Seeds ripen September–October

✔ Leaves very aromatic when rubbed between your fingers

✔ Well-drained soil is essential

✔ Slightly hairy leaves and stems

✔ Plant becomes more branched towards the top

✔ Evidence of small, purple-pink flowers

When to look for it

The best time to forage for this essential herb is during a long, hot summer (July–August), when the sun has had a chance to draw out the plant's full flavour. If you want to use the leaves dried, pick them and leave them in the shade until they are ready for the pot. In areas where the sun is less strong, try picking the leaves in that interval between the buds forming and the flowers opening.

What does it taste like?

This herb is central to so much of Mediterranean cuisine, its pungent, earthy taste and fragrance complement the sun-filled flavours of crisp, young wine, olive oil, garlic, the tangy bite of capsicum and crumbly, salt-laden cheeses.

How is it used?

Oregano is familiar to most people in its dried form, when it is used as a food flavouring for soups, stews, chicken, pork and lamb dishes, salads, risottos and tomato-based dishes – not forgetting sauces and pizzas. As well as enhancing the taste of these more delicately flavoured foods, oregano is robust enough to hold its own when coupled with garlic, chillies and onion. For the best effect, add the oregano at the end of the cooking time, briefly incorporating it before serving. Too much heat causes the herb's volatile oils to evaporate, robbing it of its flavour. You can also make a tea substitute from the dried leaves and flower stems.

Try it in

Marjoram Fish Soup (see page 231).

Common Oregano

This plant is best harvested and dried at the end of the growing season in late summer.

Papaver rhoeas

Corn poppy, field poppy

annual agricultural weed • grows well on disturbed ground •
seeds used in baking • large, showy flowers

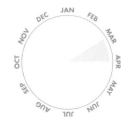

Grassland Plants

What is it?

This attractive, distinctly hairy annual is well
known for its Remembrance Day connections. It
stands 30–60 cm (12–24 in) high and has a
spread of about 15–30 cm (6–12 in).

What to look for

Multiple, erect and branching hairy stems –
often purple at the base, green towards the top

Pick corn poppy leaves early in the
season and cook them as you would
spinach, or use the leaves in salads.

– grow from a slender taproot containing a
milky sap. The pinnately divided, feather-like
leaves are alternate and about 5 cm (2 in) long.
Between June and October the plant produces
deep red to scarlet-coloured flowers, up to
10 cm (4 in) across, with a starkly contrasting
black centre. The single flowers are droopy
and nodding and made up of 4–6 petals.

Where to look

The abiding image of field poppies blooming
among the shell craters of war-torn France in the
First World War gives us a clue to the preferred
habitat of this plant – disturbed and broken
ground. Likely places to look for poppies include
ground that has been prepared for agriculture,
grassland and pastures, waste ground, field
boundaries and roadside verges. Poppies are
found throughout Europe in open, sunny sites
with moist, well-drained soil.

When to look for it

The leaves are fine to eat if foraged before the
flower buds have formed, so restrict yourself to
the spring months of March and April (check to
see that no buds are present). The flowers can
be taken throughout the season, giving you a
wide spread of months (June to October). The

seeds start to ripen from September onwards and are ready for harvesting when they change colour from green to grey or brown.

What does it taste like?

The seeds of the field poppy have a delicate, nutty flavour, compared with the more robust taste of commercial poppy seeds, which usually come from *Papaver somniferum*. This is the opium poppy, but the seeds contain none of the narcotic substances found in the sap.

How is it used?

The leaves of the corn poppy can be used raw, as a salad ingredient or cooked, treated in the same way you would spinach. Remember to pick the leaves from the plant early in the season, before the flower buds have formed. A syrup can be taken from the red poppy petals and is used as a food flavouring as well as forming a traditional drink in Mediterranean countries. It is the seeds, however, that are most often used in cooking, added as a flavouring to pastries, biscuits and breads before baking or blended with olive oil and your favourite herbs and spices as a salad dressing. Commercially, a high-quality cooking oil is extracted from the seeds. Poppy flowers have also been used for centuries as part of traditional folk medicine, principally in the treatment of coughs and to ease mild pain and nervous tension, especially with children and the elderly. The field poppy, unlike the opium poppy (*Papaver somniferum*), is not addictive.

A flavoured oil can be extracted from the poppy seeds and used as a substitute for olive oil.

Forager's checklist

- ✔ Check that seed heads are ready for picking by looking for small holes that appear just below the flat cap
- ✔ Seed heads are glabrous
- ✔ Seeds are small but produced in great numbers
- ✔ Grows only in full sunshine

Corn Poppy

Polygonum bistorta

Bistort, Easter-ledger

clump-forming perennial • good source of vitamin A • makes
a good groundcover plant • tall spikes of pink flowers

Grassland Plants

What is it?
A herbaceous perennial flowering plant. Bistort grows to 60–75 cm (24–30 in) high with a spread of up to about 50 cm (20 in).

What to look for
The root is a thick, lumpy rhizome, up to 1 m (3 ft) long, often twisted and doubled back on itself (hence the common name 'bistort'). It is black on the outside and red on the inside. Bistort produces two types of leaf. The blue-green basal leaves are broadly ovate (egg-shaped) and up to 15 cm (6 in) long. The upper leaves are distinctly triangular in shape and are held on long stalks. Tall, erect spikes of massed pink (sometimes white) flowers appear above the foliage between June and September.

Where to look
Bistort is a plant often associated with high, mountainous regions, so look for it in moist meadows and wet grassland – even in water-retentive boggy ground. It tolerates a wide range of soil types, but its preference is for acid soil in semi-shaded conditions or open ground. Bistort can be found in northern (though not the extreme north) and central Europe and the high regions of southern Europe.

When to look for it
Bistort has a long season of interest for the forager. Its semi-evergreen foliage can be taken from late winter (about March), assuming the weather is not severe, right through to the early part of autumn (September), though the earlier you pick the leaves the more tender and tastier they are (spring leaves are best). The seeds are small and fiddly and are available after ripening between August and October.

What does it taste like?
The older leaves can have a rather bitter taste, while the younger spring leaves are milder and more pleasant to eat. The leaves are a worthwhile source of vitamin A.

Young leaves should not be too chewy or bitter-tasting and can be used raw in salads or cooked as a vegetable.

How is it used?

The spring leaves of bistort can be eaten raw, as part of a salad, though some people find them a little too chewy for this purpose. Cooked, however, they make a good substitute for that much-substituted spinach. In some parts of Britain, the leaves are used as an ingredient in a bitter pudding called Easter-ledger, along with oatmeal, eggs and herbs, which is eaten during the period of Lent. You can add the seeds to salads, raw or roasted, or include them as a flavouring in sauces and dressings. Although high in tannin (removed by soaking in water followed by roasting), the roots of bistort are nutritious and good to eat. They can also be boiled or used as an ingredient in casseroles or soups.

Try it in

Bistort and Chickpea Sabzi (see page 232).

Forager's checklist

✔ Stems are unbranched
✔ Silvery hairs on the undersides of the leaves
✔ Flowers can occasionally be white
✔ Grows from a twisted, distorted rhizome

Bistort

Bold spikes of usually pink, sometimes white, flowers signal the presence of this herbaceous perennial.

Prunus domestica

Wild plum

deciduous tree growing at a medium rate • spreading habit •
often found near orchards

Grassland Plants

What is it?
This is a medium-growing deciduous tree with a
domed-to-spreading habit that reaches a height
of 10–12 m (33–40 ft) and a spread of 8–10 m
(26–33 ft).

What to look for
The bark of the wild plum is reddish-brown, and
the trunk is upright and divided. The simple
leaves are obovate (egg-shaped, but with the
narrower end at the base) to elliptical, and
about 5–7 cm (2–3 in) long. They are alternate
and the margins toothed. Small clusters of 2–3
white flowers appear between March and May,
but these are susceptible to damage by late

The obovate leaves of the wild plum
are finely and regularly serrated and
around 5–7 cm (2–3 in) long.

frosts. The wild plum is extremely similar to the
bullace (*Prunus insititia*), but its fruits are always
black and elongated, not round and various
coloured (yellow, green, red or purple), like
those of the bullace.

Where to look
This is a small tree most often found in
hedgerows and woodland or in pastures and
meadows adjacent to orchards, from where it
may have escaped from cultivation at some
point. Perhaps of Asian origin, the wild plum
is naturalized throughout Europe.

When to look for it
Spring is the time to seek out the flowers of the
wild plum, any time between March and May,
depending on location and weather, though it is
the edible fruits that attract most people, around
August and September. There is a trade-off to be
made, however, between waiting for the plums
to ripen to maximum flavour, but then suffering
the inevitable attention of birds, squirrels and
other wildlife competitors.

What does it taste like?
Depending on the precise variety of tree, the
amount of sunshine in the ripening season and

exactly when you pick your fruit, wild plums can be sharply acid or sugary sweet. The flesh can also be quite soft and granular or ripe and firm.

How is it used?

You can pick the fruit straight from the tree and eat it as a snack food. As an alternative, remove the large central stone, dice the fruit, still raw, and make a refreshing mixed fruit salad. Or you can cook the flesh to make jams, jellies and chutneys; stew it alone or with other fruit as a refreshing dessert; or use it to create rich sauces for strong-flavoured game (duck and venison). Freezes well once cooked. The flowers of the wild plum can be used as a tea substitute or used as garnish in salads, sandwiches and so on.

Try it in

Wild Plum and Almond Filo Pie (see page 233).

Caution

The wild plum belongs to a genus in which most members produce a potentially deadly poison called hydrogen cyanide. This poison is concentrated mainly in the leaves and seeds and you will immediately notice its bitter taste. However, it is usually present in such small quantities that it can do no harm. But you must not eat any seed with a particularly bitter taste or intense aroma.

Forager's checklist

✔ **White flowers composed of five petals**

✔ **Common hedgerow plant in some regions**

✔ **An edible gum can be collected from damaged areas of the trunk**

✔ **Seeds have an almond smell**

Eaten straight from the tree, the wild plum is delicious. It can also be used in jam-making and stewing.

Wild Plum

Rumex acetosa

Sorrel

inconspicuous shrub • widely distributed • arrow-shaped leaf •
ideal soup and salad ingredient • citrus flavoured

Grassland Plants

What is it?
A perennial and biennial sub-shrub. Grows to a
height of 10–30 cm (4–12 in).

What to look for
Sorrel grows in sturdy, leafy clumps. The leaves
are dull green and arrow-shaped, joining one-
third of the way down the stalk, leaving a long,
green stem. The flowers are small red-and-green
clusters tightly bunched around the top of tall
spears that appear from May to August.

Can be mistaken for
Any other member of the buckwheat family, but
notably dock plants, whose leaves are broader,
crinklier and often curled inwards, could cause
confusion with identification.

Where to look
Meadows, pastures, roadsides and heaths are
all likely habitats. Shady, damp grassland is
ideal as the leaves grow bigger. This is a
Europe-wide plant.

When to look for it
The first leaves are ready to harvest in March,
when many other green forage-foods have yet to
develop. There is little chance of finding the leaf
after mid-August.

What does it taste like?
This green leaf has a surprisingly acidic, lemony
flavour. It is particularly sharp when raw and
may be too bitter for some palates.

How is it used?
The stems, roots and seeds can be used in
infusions, but it's best to stick to the leaves.
To release the flavour, tear strips against the
grain. Some large leaves may need their stems
removed. The citrus taste makes it an excellent
addition to salads. It is halfway between a leaf

The presence of appreciable levels of
oxalic acid accounts for the distinctly
lemony flavour of the leaves.

Standing barely 30 cm (12 in) high, you need to keep a sharp eye out for the flower clusters of the sorrel plant.

vegetable and a herb and works equally well as both. When cooked it resembles spinach and is good in soups. In France, it is the chief ingredient in the popular *soup aux herbes*. As a herb sorrel adds flavour to bland, creamy dishes, ragouts and fricassees or works as a simple garnish.

Try it in
Sorrel Salad (see page 234).

Forager's checklist

✔ **Arrow-shaped green leaves**

✔ **Smooth stem**

✔ **Leaf joins stem a third of the way up**

✔ **Evidence of small red flowers**

✔ **'Veins' on leaf run at 45° to stem**

✔ **Leaves have faint lemony smell when rubbed between your fingers**

Tanacetum vulgare (syn. Chrysanthemum vulgare)

Common tansy

fragrant perennial plant • frost-tender • flowers from summer into the autumn • can be used as an insect repellent

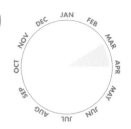

Grassland Plants

What is it?
A medium-sized perennial herb that spreads by sending out runners or by self-seeding. It stands about 1–1.5 m (3–5 ft) high and has a spread of about 75 cm (30 in).

What to look for
The stems of this attractive perennial are tall and erect and tinged a slightly reddish colour. The alternate, pinnate (feathery) leaves are finely divided and compound, 10–20 cm (4–8 in) long, approximately oblong in outline, have serrated edges and are fern-like in appearance. The golden-yellow, button-like flowers open between July and October in flat-topped terminal flower clusters.

Where to look
Common tansy grows happily in meadows, fields and hedgerows, as well as in open waste ground and grassland beside roadways and paths. It tolerates most types of soil, as well as dry or moist ground, but must have full sun. It is a widely distributed plant, growing in temperate regions throughout Europe. Tansy is a natural insect repellent and it has been planted to deter fruit flies and moths and to discourage ant infestations.

When to look for it
Tansy, which should only be eaten in moderation (see Caution below), is traditionally a herb used at Easter time (late March into April), though in some more northerly regions the leaves may not be available until well into May. Collect the new, young leaves at this time. The flowers, too, sometimes attract the attention of foragers and these are available right through to October.

What does it taste like?
Tansy is definitely an acquired taste. Popular in former times as a flavouring for egg dishes and milk puddings, the herb's pungent bitterness is not necessarily suited to the modern palate.

The pinnate (feather-like) leaves of tansy appear like those of a fern.

How is it used?

Young tansy leaves can be used in small quantities in salads or as a flavouring in milky puddings instead of nutmeg. The leaves and flower stems can be dried and used as a weak infusion and in moderation as a tea substitute. The flowers, too, make an attractive garnish. The eponymous Jack Daniels was said to have enjoyed his bourbon flavoured with sugar and a tansy leaf.

Try it in

Tansy Pudding (see page 225).

Caution

This plant should not be consumed in any form by pregnant women, as it could result in miscarriage. It contains a volatile oil high in thujone (which is also present in the alcoholic drink absinthe), a toxin that results in uterine bleeding, vomiting and convulsions if consumed in large quantities.

Forager's checklist

- ✔ **Leaves are spirally arranged**
- ✔ **Favours an open aspect**
- ✔ **Stout central stem becomes more branching towards the top**
- ✔ **Stem and branches are usually glabrous**
- ✔ **Leaves are divided into approximately seven pairs of lobes, which then divide yet again**

Common Tansy

A tall-growing, robust plant, tansy will stand up to most conditions, including strong winds.

Taraxacum officinale

Dandelion

persistent perennial weed • widely distributed • saw-toothed leaves • many varied culinary uses • can be made into beer and wine

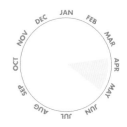

Grassland Plants

What is it?
Mostly viewed by gardeners as a persistent weed, the dandelion is a resilient hairy perennial, 5–40 cm (2–16 in) high and about 30 cm (12 in) wide.

What to look for
The dandelion grows from a deep-set taproot, any part of which left in the ground will generate a new plant. The mid-green leaves that grow from a central rosette at the base of the plant are broadly jagged. Large, bright-yellow flowers, 2.5–5 cm (1–2 in) across, are borne singly on tall, unbranched, hollow stems (standing well above the foliage) containing a milky latex sap. The seed heads that follow ripen into balls of fine wind-borne filaments, each supporting a tiny seed.

Can be mistaken for
Cat's ear (*Hypochoeris*) is also known as false dandelion, but its similarity to the dandelion is largely in the flower. The stems are branching and solid and the leaves hairier and more lobed.

Where to look
You are likely to encounter dandelions in among the grass in meadows, pastures, waste ground,

roadside verges and in your own cultivated lawns and beds at home. This is a Europe-wide plant, especially of temperate regions.

When to look for it
Apart from the very coldest months (January–February), you are likely to find dandelion leaves above ground and growing. But it is the young leaves that have the best flavour. The flowers have a very long season and apart from the coldest winter months, you are likely to find them – however, late spring is their most productive season (April–May).

The irregularly toothed leaves of the dandelion grow from a basal whirl and can be used in salads.

What does it taste like?

Older dandelion leaves are far too bitter for most palates, so people often opt for the milder-flavoured younger leaves and shoots. The root has been likened to the taste of a turnip, while the flowers are also slightly bitter.

How is it used?

Young dandelion leaves can be eaten raw as a salad vegetable and the older ones (after being steeped in water overnight) used as a cooked vegetable or included in soups. The leaves are very nutritious, containing good amounts of iron, calcium and potassium and vitamins A and C. Unopened flower buds can also be added raw to salads or the open flower heads made into a herbal tea, along with the leaves and roots. In the UK, a traditional soft drink is made from dandelion and burdock. Once ground down, the roasted root of two-year-old dandelion plants can be used as a coffee substitute. The leaves and roots together can become a flavouring for beer, and the flower heads alone are used in the production of wine.

Try it in

Dandelion Delight (see page 235).

Fully open dandelion flowers can be made into herbal tea and they are also an ingredient in wine production.

Forager's checklist

✔ Flowers close at night and open during the day

✔ Winter leaves are less bitter-tasting

✔ Surrounding grass is killed as the dandelion leaves lie flat to the ground and exclude light

✔ Roots are best collected at their fattest, in the autumn

✔ Wear gloves when picking leaves to avoid staining your skin

Wild thyme

fragrant culinary herb • ground-hugging habit • proportionately large flowers • milder flavour than cultivated forms

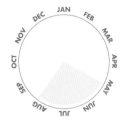

Grassland Plants

What is it?
A low, groundcover, evergreen shrub. It reaches a height of only 5–10 cm (2–4 in) and has a spread of about 30 cm (12 in).

What to look for
The tiny dark-green, ovate leaves – up to 5 mm (¼ in) long – are present year-round and grow in opposing pairs. Stems are woody, making useful sprigs to include in cooking. Heads of pinky-purple (sometimes white) flowers, large in proportion to the rest of the plant, open between May and August.

Where to look
Favouring chalk and limestone as well as light (sandy) soil, wild thyme can be found, at times in great profusion, on heathland and other grassy areas. It needs a well-drained soil and stands up to drought conditions well. To bring out the best flavour, wild thyme needs full exposure to the sun. It is naturalized throughout most of eastern, central and southern Europe.

When to look for it
The leaves of wild thyme are available for picking throughout the year, making this an

The pinky-purple heads of the flowers act as a beacon, signalling the plant's presence among its taller neighbours.

Forager's checklist

✔ **Spreads by sending out woody runners that root at the leaf joints**

✔ **Easiest to find among the grasses and other plants when in bloom**

✔ **Leaves are aromatic when rubbed between your fingers**

✔ **Flower stems up to 10 cm (4 in) tall**

✔ **Occasionally mound-forming**

Wild Thyme

Wild thyme flowers in great profusion for an extended season between late spring and late summer.

incredibly useful and flavoursome addition to mealtimes. However, if you want the bonus of its wonderful, aromatic flowers, then May–August is the peak period for foraging.

What does it taste like?
Wild thyme does not have the same intensity of taste as the cultivated form (*Thymus vulgaris*). Its flavour is more subtle and earthy and reminds your taste buds of sun-filled days and the buzz and hum of insects – even when the weather is low and gloomy.

How is it used?
You need to be heavy-handed when using wild thyme, as it does not have the same 'kick' as the cultivated form. You can use the leaves and, in season, the flower heads raw as a salad flavouring or add them to a wide range of cooked foods – from omelettes and scrambled eggs, through soups and sauces, to casseroles and roast meats. The leaves and dried flowers also make an excellent tea substitute. To dry the leaves of thyme for later use, pick them before the flowers open to capture their full intensity of flavour.

Try it in
Thyme Risotto (see page 236).

ROADSIDE PLANTS

The margins and strips of countryside adjacent to our extensive road and rail networks provide a unique environment for a variety of plant life, much of it edible. Trees and shrubs and a host of annuals, biennials, perennials all find a niche where they flourish, often in sight of the travelling public yet in ground that is largely undisturbed for most of the time. And not only wild plants enjoy this habitat – as transport routes developed, encouraging the spread of habitation along the way, many cultivated plants made their escape, establishing colonies and outposts in the surrounding countryside.

Armoracia rusticana

Horseradish

invasive herbaceous perennial • widely distributed • root can be
sliced or grated • long stems of white flowers

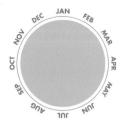

What is it?

A medium-sized herbaceous perennial growing
to 75–90 cm (30–35 in) that will effectively fill
any amount of available free space unless
regularly harvested.

What to look for

The shiny green basal leaves of horseradish
are large, dock-like, ovate to oblong in shape,
and about 50 cm (20 in) long. The taproot, for
which horseradish is so prized, is usually stout,
unbranched and fleshy, up to 60 cm (24 in)
long and 5 cm (2 in) thick. The flowers, which
appear in May through September in terminal
panicles on tall spikes well above the basal
leaves, are white with four petals measuring
about 5 mm (¼ in) long.

Where to look

Horseradish flourishes on poor ground,
neglected waste land, abandoned gardens,
brick-strewn demolition sites, railway
embankments and the hard, compacted soil
typically found on roadside verges. It likes deep,
well-drained soil and not too much water. It will
tolerate light, dappled shade, but does best in
full sun. Probably originating around the
Mediterranean region and Turkey, horseradish is

naturalized throughout Europe, having escaped
from cultivation during the 2,000 years it has
been grown.

Horseradish leaves are large, robust-
looking and prominently veined,
growing straight out of the ground.

When to look for it

Horseradish is fully hardy and so is available for harvesting the whole year round. Alternatively, once the leaves have died down and the seed has set, in late autumn or early winter (around December), dig the roots up for immediate use. If you cannot easily get back to the site to harvest more as required, dig up excess roots and store them in dry sand to preserve their flavour.

What does it taste like?

Do not be fooled by the mild aroma coming from the roots – peel off the brown outer layer and slice or grate the white inner flesh and you will be hit by its pungent smell and fiery, mustardy flavour.

How is it used?

To prepare the root, soak in water for an hour or two before cleaning; scrape off the outer brown layer, leaving the flesh exposed. To make horseradish sauce you grate the root, combining it with mustard, vinegar and various seasonings. Try adding grated horseradish to yogurt, mayonnaise or cream cheese and serving it as a sauce with meat and fish dishes. You can also slice it very thinly and simply eat it on bread and butter. In some regions, the root is cut into chunks and roasted like a parsnip. Roasting will reduce its impact as it destroys the volatile oil that accounts for its flavour. The young leaves make an interesting addition to the salad bowl, but use them in moderation or their flavour will dominate. Finally, sprouted horseradish seeds are another salad idea.

Horseradish

Forager's checklist

- ✔ Pungent smell when leaves are rubbed between your fingers
- ✔ Bright green leaves are very large and become obvious in early to mid-summer
- ✔ Take a spade to help you dislodge the deep-set roots
- ✔ You may be reduced to tears while preparing the root, like chopping onions

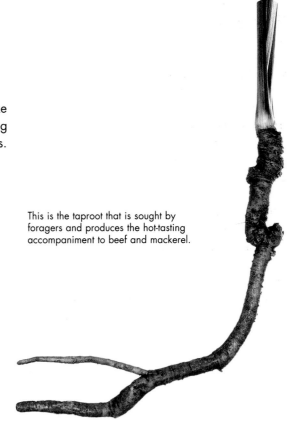

This is the taproot that is sought by foragers and produces the hot-tasting accompaniment to beef and mackerel.

Anthriscus sylvestris

Cow parsley

early-flowering biennial • requires careful identification •
feathery, fern-like leaves • used in salads and as a food
flavouring

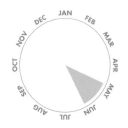

What is it?
A medium- to tall-growing biennial plant, about
60–120 cm (2–4 ft) or more, with a spread of
about 60 cm (24 in).

What to look for
Cow parsley is an upright plant with a tall,
green, furrowed stem, slightly hairy towards the
bottom; its mid- to dark-green leaves are very
divided, giving a feathery, fern-like appearance.
The leaves are triangular, 15–30 cm (6–12 in)
long. In spring to early summer (April–June),
cow parsley produces umbrella-shaped clusters
(umbels) of small white flowers, each about 4
mm (⅙ in) across.

Can be mistaken for
You must take great care in identifying cow
parsley, as it is very similar in appearance
to the deadly poisonous hemlock (*Conium
maculatum*). Both plants belong to the family
of aromatic herbs *Umbelliferae*, but cow parsley
does not match hemlock's 2 m (6½ ft) plus
height. Hemlock also has a distinctive 'rodent'
or 'mousy' type of aroma and its stems are
blotched with purple. If your identification
is at all uncertain, pass on this one.

Where to look
Pastures, hedgerows and lightly wooded areas
just about anywhere in Europe, are likely to be
host to at least a few examples of cow parsley.
However, it is also extremely common along the
sides of footpaths through woods or waste
ground and smothering the verges of our roads
and motorways.

When to look for it
Assuming your identification is certain (see
above), pick fresh, new leaves of cow parsley
throughout its growing season, although the
early-season growth (May–June) has a better
flavour and is not as bitter as later-season
leaves. The stems die back in late summer, and

Very divided and essentially triangular
in shape, the leaves of cow parsley are
delicate-looking, feathery and fern-like.

a new crop of non-flowering stems and leaves appears in autumn, which stays green throughout the winter.

What does it taste like?

Another common name for cow parsley is wild chervil, which gives you a clue to its flavour, which is described as being sharp and fresh with subtle overtones of carrot. This plant is best eaten raw, as cooking quickly weakens its taste to the point of invisibility.

How is it used?

You can use cow parsley as an effective substitute for cultivated chervil, as a flavouring in soups, salads and sauces and as a garnish for freshly boiled potatoes, cold potato salad, as a flavouring for tomato and cucumber combinations, and in egg dishes.

Forager's checklist

✔ **After the flowers, it produces oblong-shaped black fruit, about 5 mm (¼ in) long**

✔ **Seeds are produced from July onwards**

✔ **Stem is hollow and branched**

✔ **Leaves are slightly hairy**

✔ **The plant is not aromatic**

Cow Parsley

Part of the same plant family as poisonous hemlock, cow parsley does not reach its lethal relative's height of more than 2 m (6½ ft).

Artemisia vulgaris

Mugwort

herbaceous perennial • densely clustered flower heads • angular stems •associates well with fatty foods

What is it?
A medium to tall herbaceous perennial herb, 60–100 cm (2–3 ft) tall, with a spread of 45–75 cm (18–30 in).

What to look for
Growing from a woody root, the erect stems of mugwort have a reddy-purplish tinge. The leaves are dark green, divided into jagged leaflets, giving them a pinnate (feather-like) appearance, and up to 20 cm (8 in) long. The undersides of the leaves have a dense covering of white hairs. Densely clustered, branched heads of reddish or pale yellow tubular flowers open in succession from July to September.

Where to look
The best places to find mugwort are in meadows, hedgerows, waste ground, railway embankments and roadside verges. Mugwort is drought-tolerant and prefers a well-drained, acid soil, but it will also grow in alkaline soil. It does best in full sun or dappled or very open shade. It is native to the temperate regions of Europe.

When to look for it
Collect the leaves in spring (March–April), taking advantage of the fresh, new growth. The flowers are also collected (see below) and you can take these any time during the flowering season (July–September).

What does it taste like?
The overwhelming taste of mugwort is bitter. It is often used as an aid to digestion and so is included in moderation with other herbs for this purpose. It must be said that it is not to everybody's liking.

The young spring shoots and leaves can be cooked along with fatty foods to add flavour and aid the digestion.

Forager's checklist

✔ Leaves are aromatic when rubbed between your fingers
✔ Stems are thin and hairless
✔ Lower leaves are shaped like a lyre
✔ Flowers are arranged in oval-shaped heads

How is it used?

Use the leaves of mugwort raw, especially the fresh spring growth, as a salad ingredient, but the taste is distinctly bitter and so exercise restraint. It is thought to be excellent for the digestion, however, which accounts for its traditional use as an accompaniment to such fatty foods as duck, goose, pork, mutton and eel. Mugwort flowers were once widely used as a flavouring in beer, but fell out of favour when hops were introduced. The Japanese use mugwort as a flavouring in a glutinous type of rice dumpling.

Caution

Mugwort contains a toxic substance called thujone, which is not normally present in sufficient quantities to be harmful. However, pregnant women, in particular, should avoid eating this herb in large quantities.

Mugwort

Mugwort's requirement for well-drained soil and its drought-tolerance make it an ideal roadside plant.

Wild asparagus

drooping, fern-like perennial • gourmet-quality vegetable • male and female plants • delicate flavour

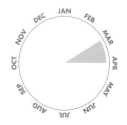

What is it?
This medium to tall fern-like perennial reaches 1.5–2 m (5–6½ ft) with a spread of about 75 cm (30 in)

What to look for
The leaves of wild asparagus are much reduced and are more like scales than true leaves, about 5 mm (¼ in) long coming from the multi-branched stems. Although the tall, glabrous (hairless) stems are upright, the long branches give the plant a delicate, drooping appearance. Between May and August scattered, bell-shaped, whitish-green flowers appear, single or paired, from the leaf axils (the junctions where the branches leave the stem). These are followed by red berries.

Where to look
Despite its rather delicate appearance, wild asparagus is a tough and resilient plant, well able to cope with the unpromising conditions on waste ground, disturbed sites, railway embankments and roadside verges. Apart from requiring a moist, well-drained soil, it does best in full sun. Asparagus is native to Europe, especially temperate western Europe.

When to look for it
You need a good eye to find wild asparagus when it is at its best for picking. Unfortunately, when you see its distinctive fern-like foliage you know you have left it too late, as it is the young shoots (or spears) that are the gourmet's delight. Wild asparagus starts to grow very early in the spring, so begin looking March–April time. Look for the tall, withered stems of last year's growth among other vegetation. New spears will appear throughout the summer months (if rainfall is good), and the more you pick, the more you encourage new shoots to push up and break through the soil (take this too far, however, and you will weaken the plant for next year).

Succulent spears of wild asparagus should be ready for picking around March and April.

What does it taste like?

With asparagus, the fattest shoots have the best flavour, which is described as fresh, oniony, grassy, nutty or sweet. Some people find the taste somewhat 'clinical'. This might have something to do with asparagus's ability to turn urine slightly yellow-green in colour produce a very strong odour, which some people can detect.

How is it used?

The very best asparagus shoots (spears) are spring-harvested; use these cut up raw in salads, though they are most often steamed or lightly boiled and served with freshly ground black pepper and a generous knob of butter. The seeds can be roasted and used as a coffee substitute. Undersized or broken spears that might look less than wonderful on the plate should not be wasted, as they are perfect for turning into asparagus soup, sliced and quickly stir-fried as an accompaniment to shrimps or chicken, or cooked as part of a chicken and asparagus pie. This vegetable also associates well with egg dishes, giving a superb flavour to the traditional bacon quiche.

Try it in

Grilled Asparagus (see page 237).

Forager's checklist

✔ Grows from a long rhizome

✔ Spears start in early spring

✔ Seeds ripen between September and October

✔ Roadside asparagus could be susceptible to pollution from car exhausts

The fern-like plumes of foliage may be attractive, but they are a sign that you have left it too late for foraging.

Wild Asparagus

Borago officinalis

Borage

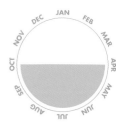

drought-tolerant • good source of potassium and calcium • widely distributed • adds flavour and colour to food and drink

What is it?
A bushy annual herb with prominent, bristly hairs over the stems and leaves. It reaches a height of 30–60 cm (12–24 in) and has a spread of 15–30 cm (6–12 in).

What to look for
The alternate-growing, oval-shaped leaves are deep green, big and wrinkled, 5–15 cm (2–6 in) long, with wavy margins. The branched stems are round and hollow. For most of the summer (June–October), borage supports very attractive bright-blue flowers consisting of five reflexed (backward-pointing), triangular-shaped petals and prominent black, cone-shaped anthers.

Where to look
Borage is a frequent escapee from cultivation and is often found following the main roads across most of the European continent. Some sources give central Europe as its place of origin, while others quote Syria. Borage is also found on waste ground and, while not being fussy about its environment and tolerating poor-quality soil, it grows into a bushier, more productive plant on nutritionally rich ground. It does best in full sun where it receives some protection from winds.

When to look for it
Pick the leaves and flowers throughout its lengthy growing season – from late April for the leaves and from June for the flowers – right through to October. You could try growing a few borage plants indoors on a sunny window sill.

Borage flowers make an eye-catching garnish and you can also use the candied flowers as cake decorations.

What does it taste like?

The overwhelming flavour of borage is the refreshing summer taste of cucumber, with a slightly salty tang to the leaves. The taste of the flowers, which are also used, especially in drinks and beverages (see below), is of slightly sweetened cucumber.

How is it used?

Use the leaves of borage either raw or cooked, but bear in mind that they are very bristly and may not be to everybody's liking. To overcome this, cut them up quite small before adding to salads, soups and stews (add them near the end of the cooking time to preserve their flavour). The raw leaves are also perfect in Pimms, the quintessential summer drink. Or try mixing a generous handful of finely chopped borage leaves with cabbage and then steam briefly. Borage's blue flowers make an attractive garnish for fruit punch, or freeze the flowers into ice cubes and serve with gin-based cocktails and mixers. The flowers can be candied and used as cake decorations. Finally, the leaves, stems and flowers make a refreshing tea substitute.

Try it in

Borage Tart (see page 238).

Caution

Borage contains small amounts of an alkaloid that could, if eaten to excess, be detrimental to the liver in some people. If you have any form of liver problem it may be wise not to eat borage.

Forager's checklist

✔ Has an untidy, straggling habit
✔ Seeds ripen between July and October
✔ Hairy stems and leaves
✔ Attractive to bees and makes good honey

Borage

This plant has traditionally been used in medicine to help ease the effects of melancholia and lift the mood.

Brassica nigra

Black mustard

tall, spindly annual • used as a spice for 5,000 years • tolerant of different growing conditions • valued for its heat and pungency

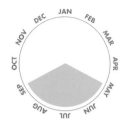

What is it?
This thin-stemmed, spindly annual often topples over at the end of the season when it is heavy with fruits. It reaches a height of 1.2 m (4 ft), and has a spread of about 60 cm (24 in).

What to look for
The lower leaves of this multi-branched, fast-growing annual herb have 1–3 lateral lobes and a larger terminal lobe. The upper leaves are more oblong in shape, unlobed, coarsely toothed, glaucous (powdery-looking) below and dark green above; all leaves are alternate and deep green. Between June and August, elongated racemes of small, yellow, four-petalled flowers, about 1 cm (½ in) across, appear on the upper stems above the foliage. Seed pods follow.

Where to look
Wild mustard is a common escapee from cultivation and often follows the route of major transport routes. It can also be found on all types of waste ground and in fields and meadows. It is considered a weed on cultivated land. It is thought to have originated in the Mediterranean region or perhaps the Near East, but is now commonly found in central, southern and all temperate regions of Europe.

When to look for it
The leaves of black mustard are available May–September, although most people value this plant for its seeds. The seed pods, which you will find hard up against the stem, ripen July–September.

What does it taste like?
The leaves of black mustard are hot and pungent-tasting, while the flavour of the seeds, once prepared (see below), is even more so. Black mustard is more pungent than either

Lightly boil the leaves of black mustard, as you would spinach, or use them raw as a salad ingredient.

Forager's checklist

✔ **Tolerates a coastal environment**

✔ **Grows from a taproot**

✔ **Lower leaves hairy**

✔ **Leaves have pungent aroma**

✔ **Long, thin stems**

brown mustard (*Brassica juncea*), which is also known as Indian mustard, or white mustard (*Sinapis alba*).

How is it used?

Use the leaves of black mustard, raw or cooked, whenever you want to add a touch of heat and exotic spice to your cooking. Finely chopped leaves are perfect as a salad ingredient (adjust the quantity depending on the level of heat you want); they can also be treated like spinach. The young flowering stems can also be lightly boiled to make a cooked vegetable. To use the seeds, you can either sprinkle them on the top of, for example, cheese before grilling it, or grind them down into mustard powder (which is a key ingredient in curry powder). Mixing the mustard powder with a little cold water (to form a thick paste) produces the hottest results; mixing it with hot water or vinegar gives a milder, more bitter, flavour.

Black Mustard

This rather untidy, undistinguished plant can be found on all types of waste ground, including roadside verges.

Chenopodium bonus-henricus

Good King Henry

medium-growing annual herb • widely distributed • used as a
food source by early man • excellent source of vitamin B

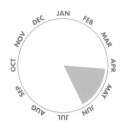

What is it?
Though never making a large plant, this annual
(sometimes perennial) is variable in height,
depending on conditions, 30–75 cm (12–30 in),
with a spread of 30–60 cm (12–24 in).

What to look for
The dark-green leaves of Good King Henry
are 5–10 cm (2–4 in) long, coarsely toothed
or undulate, broadly triangular to diamond
shaped, often with two lobes near the stem,
giving them a goosefoot appearance. The
flowers appear May–August on tall, nearly
bare spikes held well clear of the foliage.
Each flower is only about 2.5–4 mm (⅛ in)
across, yellowy-green. The seeds that follow
are more reddish and only about 2 mm (¹⁄₁₆ in).

Where to look
This is a plant of pastures, farmyards and
manure heaps, as well as roadside verges,
in any ground that is especially rich in nitrogen.
Requiring a moist, well-drained soil, it grows
well in full sunshine or in open, dappled
shade. Good King Henry is found through
most of Europe, including Scandinavia, and
was introduced into Britain with the Romans
2,000 years ago.

When to look for it
Be careful not to take too greedily from a single
plant or you will weaken it. When you find a
clump of plants growing wild, pick just a little
from each. The foraging season for Good King
Henry begins in mid-spring and lasts until early
summer (late April–June). The new shoots
coming through then are best picked when
about 20 cm (8 in) long. After this time, allow
the new shoots to grow to maturity. The leaves

The broadly triangular leaves of Good
King Henry make it one of the easiest
of the goosefoots to recognize.

can be harvested from late spring (May) through to mid-summer (August), after which they become too tough and bitter.

What does it taste like?

The young spring leaves have the mildest flavour, similar to spinach, but there is no denying that even the young leaves may be too bitter for some tastes. The young shoots are most often likened to asparagus, but without the subtlety of that most excellent vegetable.

How is it used?

The peculiar name of this plant came about, so the story goes, to distinguish it from a poisonous species, known as Bad Henry, which grew in association with it in the wild, though looking nothing like it. You can eat the leaves raw (sparingly) in salads to add a slight edge to what is often a rather bland selection of salad leaves, or cook them as you would spinach. The new shoots are best bundled together, like asparagus, and lightly boiled for a few minutes until tender and served with freshly ground black pepper and melted butter.

Try it in

Good King Henry's Nuts (see page 239).

Forager's checklist

✔ Stems are hollow
✔ Seeds ripen July–September
✔ Slight waxy feel to the leaves
✔ Leaves wilt quickly after picking
✔ Reddish tinge to new foliage

Good King Henry

The cooked flower buds have an excellent flavour. Allow some flowers to set seed to ensure the plant's future.

Primula veris

Cowslip

low-growing wildflower • bright yellow blooms • once commonly used in wine-making • can be densely clump-forming

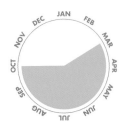

What is it?
A low-growing perennial, 10–30 cm (4–12 in) high, with a spread of about 20 cm (8 in).

What to look for
The leaves of this low-growing, hairy perennial form a rosette at the base of the plant. The leaves are narrower at the base, 5–15 cm (2–6 in) long and 2.5–6 cm (1–2½ in) wide. Between April and May, cheerful, yellow, fragrant flowers open in clusters of 10–30 blooms on a single stem about 10–20 cm (4–8 in) tall. Each flower is about 1.5 cm (¾ in) across.

Can be mistaken for
The cowslip can be confused with its near relative, the oxlip (*Primula elatior*). Although generally similar in appearance, the oxlip has larger, paler-yellow flowers. There are no known hazards associated with this plant and its leaves are also edible.

Where to look
Chalky soil, downs, meadow land, hedgerows and railway embankments are all likely places to find cowslips. Look in the dappled shade of woodland edges as well as in open ground in full sun. Cowslips are also used as a landscaping plant, planted in large numbers on

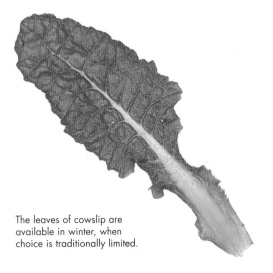

The leaves of cowslip are available in winter, when choice is traditionally limited.

Forager's checklist

✔ Grows from a short, stout rhizome

✔ Leaves ovate to oblong in shape

✔ Flowers sweetly fragrant, with orange spots

✔ Given the right conditions, cowslips spread to form dense clumps embankments fringing motorways and other major road systems. Cowslip is common throughout Europe, though in some regions the plant has come under severe pressure from changes in land use, the use of herbicides and over-collection from the wild.

When to look for it
The leaves of cowslip are available for picking very early in the season, from late winter or early spring (around March) onwards (until about October). Time your visits more carefully for the flowers, however, as the season is not very long (April–May).

What does it taste like?
The virtue of the leaves lies mainly in the fact that they are available very early in the year, rather than their taste, which is unremarkable. The flowers, however, once processed, have a sweetly fragrant flavour.

How is it used?
The younger the leaves, the better they are raw in salads, though you will probably want to use them for a little bulk rather than as the dominant leaf. They can also be chopped and used, fresh or dried, as a tea substitute. Try adding cowslip leaves to a selection of other herbs as a stuffing for meat and poultry. The bright yellow flowers make a perfect garnish for a range of salads and cooked dishes, and you can also cook them as part of a conserve. In the past, when the cowslip was a more common wildflower, they were harvested in great numbers to make cowslip wine.

Cowslip

Umbels of large flowers open on stems well above the foliage, among neighbouring plants and grasses.

Stellaria media

Chickweed

forms invasive, loosely growing mats • grows year-round •
a source of vitamins and minerals • all parts are edible

What is it?
This low-growing annual has weak, straggly stems
that tend to trail along without gaining much
height, creating effective groundcover. It might
struggle to form a mat about 12 cm (5 in) off the
ground with a spread of about 50 cm (20 in).

What to look for
The leaves of chickweed are opposite growing,
mid- to yellow-green and ovate. Apart from
some of the upper leaves, they are attached
to the thin, trailing, rather fragile stems by
hairy petioles. Look carefully and you will see
a line of fine hairs down one side of the stems,
switching sides at every node. Showy, star-
shaped white flowers can be found in bloom
throughout the year.

Where to look
You are likely to find chickweed growing just
about anywhere, in grassland (where it will
compete with established species), waste
ground, roadside verges, cultivated fields and
garden beds. It is an invasive weed and is not
only widespread throughout Europe, but is found
in most regions of the world. The only conditions
that defeat it are heat and lack of water – it
much prefers the cool and damp.

When to look for it
Although an annual plant, chickweed often
germinates in the autumn (as well as the rest of
the year) and so is available in winter, until
knocked back by the onset of hard frosts
(January–February). Its year-round availability is
helped by its ability to flower and set seed at
the same time. This nutritious plant is ideal for
foraging and the only time it is really not worth
picking is in the height of summer between July
and September, when it is limp with the heat
and struggling to cope.

This tough, self-fertilizing, groundcover
plant grows in most conditions and can
be picked throughout the year.

Forager's checklist

- ✔ White flower petals are deeply lobed, making the five petals look like ten
- ✔ Seed leaves have very prominent mid-veins
- ✔ Stems are mostly prostrate
- ✔ Flowers are about 6 mm (¼ in) across
- ✔ Leaves fold over to protect growing tips at night

What does it taste like?

Some people report that the leaves and stems (the leaves are too small to pick off the stems) of chickweed are too bitter to use raw in salads, while others combine them with wild chervil and a good crisp eating apple, adding seasoning and an oil-and-vinegar dressing. Once cooked, it is difficult to distinguish the taste of chickweed from early-cropping spinach.

How is it used?

Chickweed is a good source of vitamin C as well as containing vitamins A, B1 and B2. It also contains magnesium, iron, calcium and potassium, among others. The leaves and stems can be used raw in salads or cooked and treated like spinach (see above). The seeds, if you have the patience to gather enough, can be ground down and used as a thickening agent in soups or added to flour when making bread.

The stems, leaves and flowers can all be picked and used to make a nutritious salad or cooked as a vegetable.

SEASIDE PLANTS

We focus now on seaside plants – not only those adapted to live by the sea, but also some of the seaweeds that we might normally ignore, washed up on the beach or growing in rockpools and on rocks exposed at low tide. Many of these maritime dwellers are both delicious and highly nutritious, packed with vitamins and essential minerals. Sea kale, for example, we know was taken in pickled form on long sea voyages by the ancient Romans because it helped prevent illness among the crew, and in this way earned one of its other common names – scurvy grass.

Beta vulgaris ssp. *maritima*

Sea beet, sea spinach

large, fleshy leaves • known in Britain since Roman times •
flowers open throughout summer • delicious-tasting vegetable

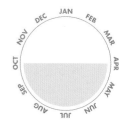

What is it?
An untidy, sprawling annual or perennial herb that reaches a height of about 1–1.2 m (3–4 ft).

What to look for
The shiny, dark-green leaves of sea beet are larger and thicker than you might expect for a wild vegetable and the lower ones have a prominent mid-rib. The stems and flower spike display a flush of red. The flower spike is wavy rather than straight and tiny yellow-green flowers, without petals or stalks, open (in groups of 1–4 blooms) between June and September.

Where to look
The most likely place to find sea beet is along the coast – nestling into sand dunes, pushing up through the loose shingle, or fighting for a foothold on sea walls and cliff edges – anywhere, in fact, with a patch of bare, open ground in full sunshine. Where conditions are right, you are likely to find good-sized colonies of wind-pollinated sea beet, which is thought to be the wild ancestor of today's cultivated beet species (sugar beet, fodder beet, yellow beet, beetroot and Swiss chard). It is native to most of the temperate regions of Europe and especially the Mediterranean area.

When to look for it
The edible part of this plant is the leaves and the best season is April–October, though if you live in milder areas, you should be able to find leaves to pick throughout the year. Show some restraint in the winter, however, if you want the clump to survive and recover in the spring.

What does it taste like?
The leaves are spinach-like in flavour, though perhaps a little less intense than the cultivated varieties you are accustomed to, and with a slightly salty taste. Like spinach, it reduces hugely when cooked, so make sure you pick sufficient.

Clean the leaves thoroughly, using the young ones raw in salads and the older, tougher ones for cooking.

Shingle beds make an ideal site for this seaside plant, as do sand dunes, sea walls and, as here, cliff tops.

Forager's checklist

✔ **Remove the prominent mid-rib of large leaves before cooking**

✔ **May and June are the tastiest months for the leaves**

✔ **Upper leaves are more spear-shaped**

✔ **Flowers are up to 8 mm (⅓ in) across**

✔ **Floppy leaves with untoothed margins**

How is it used?

You can eat the fleshy leaves raw, chopped up as a salad ingredient. Early-season leaves are best for this as they are more tender and less bitter than the late-season leaves, especially those picked in very hot weather. The larger, more leathery leaves are best boiled, as you would spinach, in a little water. Don't overcook them. When done, force as much water as possible from the leaves and toss them while still steaming hot in unsalted butter and add freshly ground black pepper. Reserve the nutrient-rich cooking water for use as stock.

Try it in

Sea Beet Cannelloni (see page 241).

Chondrus crispus

Irish moss, carragheen

multi-branched seaweed • good source of vitamins and minerals •
widely used as a food thickener • can be dried for later use

Seaside Plants

What is it?
This species of purplish-red seaweed (not a moss at all, despite its common name) produces bunches of multi-branched fronds up to about 15–20 cm (6–8 in) long.

What to look for
When alive and growing well, Irish moss has a disc-shaped holdfast by which it attaches itself to the rock or other hard substrate, and when seen under water in good light its colour can be iridescent. In very strong light, however, it can appear green. Growing from a narrow, unbranched stem (or stipe), the essentially wide, flat fronds branch and branch again to form a fan shape.

Where to look
Irish moss is found growing in abundance in the tidal zone of the middle to lower rocky shoreline and in flooded rock pools. It is widely distributed around the Atlantic coastline of Europe. It will tolerate a certain range of salinities and so you may also find it growing in estuaries – although it will not grow in brackish water.

When to look for it
The best time to forage for this seaweed is in mid- to late spring (April–May) when the fronds are young and fresh and have not taken too much of a beating from the waves. These fronds are also the best ones to dry for later use, though fronds taken at other times of the year are perfectly acceptable.

What does it taste like?
Since Irish moss is principally used for the production of carrageenan, a thickening agent, its taste is rather gelatinous.

The vegetarian gelatine from this seaweed can be used in aspic, jelly and cheese, or in soups and stews.

Forager's checklist

✔ Sometimes brown-red in colour

✔ Plant segments are usually wedge-shaped

✔ Dry plant in the sun for later use (wetting occasionally with clean water)

✔ Very variable in shape, depending on water depth and wave action

✔ Can be steamed and eaten as a fresh vegetable

How is it used?

You can use Irish moss, either fresh or dried, to make a type of vegetarian gelatine. Simmer the cleaned seaweed gently in water or milk (1:3 by volume), with sugar and flavourings to suit, until the seaweed has mostly dissolved. Remove any remaining fragments, pour the liquid into a mould to set, and you will then have a nutritious source of vitamins A and B1, as well as iron, bromine and protein. This gelatine is now suitable for use in making soft cheeses, blancmange, ice cream, jelly, aspic and so on. You can also add it to soups, stews and puddings. When dried, the seaweed loses most of its colour, becoming a rather translucent light yellow, For cooking purposes, however, you can use the dried material just as you would the fresh.

Irish Moss

Look on rocks left exposed at low tide or in flooded rock pools on the shoreline for the fronds of Irish moss.

Foeniculum vulgare

Fennel

glabrous perennial herb • flowers from summer into autumn •
strong smell of liquorice • all parts of the plant can be eaten

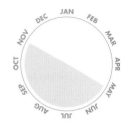

What is it?
A solid, upright, tall-growing perennial herb
(evergreen) that reaches 1.5–2 m (5–6½ ft),
sometimes 2.5 m (8 ft), with a spread of 1 m
(3 ft) or more.

What to look for
The soft, pinnate (feathery) leaves of this bluish-
green plant are triangular in shape, each
segment almost hair- or thread-like and about
5 cm (2 in) long. The stems and leaves have
a strong, sweet smell of liquorice. Loosely
arranged flat-topped umbels of golden-yellow
flowers are in bloom between July and October.
These are followed by seeds.

Can be mistaken for
Fennel can be confused with the toxic poison
hemlock (*Conium maculatum*), which looks
very similar, and tends to grow in boggy or
poorly drained ground. To tell them apart,
crush some leaves in your hand and smell –
fennel is distinctly liquorice or aniseed, while
hemlock is musty and mousy.

Where to look
Fennel is commonly found growing on waste
ground, roadside verges, cliffs and in damp

Pick the young growing tips for the
best flavour. The leaves also make an
attractive garnish for foods and soups.

Forager's checklist

✔ **Leaves are strongly aromatic when
crushed between your fingers**

✔ **Tiny individual flowers just 2 mm (¹⁄₁₆ in)
across or smaller**

✔ **Seeds ripen from September and into
November**

✔ **On a hot day you can smell the aniseed
aroma of the plant before you touch it**

areas often near the coast. It requires full sun to do well and well-drained soil. It is now naturalized in Britain and is widespread throughout southern Europe.

When to look for it
Collect the seeds of fennel in very early November – try to get them before they are fully ripe and dried out. You can forage for the leaves any time between May and November, though, as with most vegetables, the younger leaves are more tender and have the best flavour.

What does it taste like?
The aroma of this plant is so powerfully aromatic that you taste exactly what you smell – aniseed or sweet liquorice. Apart from the obvious, fennel also has a fresh nuttiness as well as hints of tarragon and chervil.

How is it used?
Chop the young foliage up for salads; large sprigs of the lacy foliage make an attractive garnish on a range of cooked dishes. The leaves and seeds, used separately or in combination, make a popular tea substitute, and the sprouted seeds are a great addition to salads. Use the seeds as a flavouring in cakes and breads as well as to liven up the taste of sausages. The leaves are often used as an accompaniment to fish dishes, but try them with cheese dips and soups as well. And don't forget the root, which you can cook as you would a parsnip.

Try it in
Finocchio Fennel (see page 242).

Fennel

The flowers should be over by October and the seeds ready for collection by about the beginning of November.

Crambe maritima

Sea kale

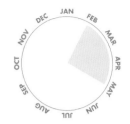

low-growing perennial • grows from a branched rhizome •
pickled leaves used by the Romans • older leaves can become
bitter-tasting

Seaside Plants

What is it?
This fleshy-leaved perennial plant is low-growing, reaching a height of up to 60 cm (24 in), with a similar spread.

What to look for
An erect stem, 2–3 cm (about 1 in) wide, growing from a fleshy, branched rhizome, with large lower leaves and smaller upper ones, from purple leaf stalks, first alerts you to the presence of sea kale. The bluish-green, hairless lower leaves are ovate (egg-shaped), about 25–35 cm (10–14 in) long, and have a glaucous (frosted) appearance. The heavy, fleshy leaves are deeply cut and have wavy margins. Clusters of sweet-smelling white flowers open June–August.

Where to look
Sea kale, as you would expect from its common name, is a coastal, seaside plant, growing in both sandy soil and poking up through shingle or loose pebbles, along much of the northern and western seaboards of Europe where the climate is cool and damp. It is not a native of the Mediterranean. It tolerates poor-quality ground, is drought-tolerant and will grow in saline soil. Its preference is for open, light shade or full sun.

When to look for it
The tastiest leaves are available early in the season (February–May). The older leaves can be quite bitter and not nearly as pleasant. Another period of interest for the forager is around May–June, before the flower buds open – you can steam the flowering stems (still in bud) or use the unopened flower buds raw (see below).

The bluish-green, wavy-edged leaves are unlikely to be mistaken for any other plant growing on the shoreline.

What does it taste like?

The young leaves and shoots of sea kale have a pleasant crispness, if not overcooked, and a nutty flavour – a taste that some people liken to hazelnuts, but with a hint of bitterness.

How is it used?

Use the young leaves and shoots raw in mixed salads or lightly boiled or steamed as you would asparagus. Drain the water after cooking and throw in some butter to melt and freshly ground black pepper before serving. Once the flowering shoots have reached about 15 cm (6 in) in length, but before the flower buds have opened, lightly cook them as you would sprouting broccoli. The fleshy rhizome is edible and is rich in both sugars and starch. This plant can also be pickled for long-term preservation. The Romans used pickled sea kale on long sea journeys to prevent scurvy – hence one of its common names, scurvy grass. Sea kale is under threat from coastline changes, so take only a little from each plant in order to preserve it for future years.

Try it in

Sea Kale Salad (see page 243).

Forager's checklist

- ✔ Often found growing in clumps
- ✔ Can be found very close to the sea
- ✔ After flowering, globular seeds develop inside a woody seed case
- ✔ Favours rocky places to grow, such as cliffs and sea walls, as well as sand dunes
- ✔ Flowers have four petals and are sweet-smelling

Sea Kale

Treat the older leaves as you would cabbage, while the younger leaves can be lightly boiled or steamed.

Porphyra umbilicalis

Purple laver

leaf-like thallus • highly nutritious seaweed • colour variable •
easily recognized growing on seashore rocks

Seaside Plants

What is it?
Thin, gelatinous sheets of seaweed just a single cell thick, comprising different-shaped fronds or blades. Individual plants are about 20–25 cm (8–10 in) in diameter.

What to look for
The thallus (a plant body that does not have a vascular system, stem, roots or leaves) of purple laver is flattened, and its species name, *umbilicalis*, comes from the Latin meaning 'of the navel'. This is a reference to its, usually central, holdfast and the pinched appearance of the surrounding membrane. Laver is usually green when young and becomes more purple or reddish-brown as it matures.

The reddish-brown colour of this example of purple laver indicates that it is from a mature specimen.

Where to look
Look for purple laver clinging by its holdfast to rocks, mooring buoys, large stones, sea walls and wharf supports in protected waters and somewhere it is likely to accumulate a covering of sand. Widely distributed around the Atlantic and North Sea coastlines of Europe.

When to look for it
The best time to forage for purple laver is from early spring to about the middle of the season – from March to the end of April. This is when laver is most tender and by far the best-tasting.

Forager's checklist

✔ **Laver turns green when it is toasted**

✔ **Avoid very sandy patches as they require extensive cleaning**

✔ **Grows on the area of shoreline that is covered by the tide**

✔ **Different species of *Porphyra* often grow intermingled, and all can be mixed and used together**

By the time summer is upon you, the fronds have toughened up considerably. To harvest this nutritious product, all you need do is wait for the tide to turn and then pick the exposed seaweed from its support.

What does it taste like?

Judged by some to taste like sludge, while others can't sing its praises loudly enough. Some claim it is an appetite stimulant, while others say it has the mild flavour of fibrous fish: 'what fish might taste like if it grew out of the ground'. Most of the salt is washed out of the laver before it is cooked, so the finished product is low in sodium.

How is it used?

You can air dry laver – strung up on a clothes line in the sunshine or toasted over a fire – and use it as a flavouring agent in soups, sauces and stews. To make the famous Welsh laver bread, break sheets of cleaned seaweed up into large pieces and simmer it gently in a pan of lightly salted water for at least four hours (make sure it does not boil dry or stick to the sides). You will know when it is cooked, as the sheets will have broken down into a coarse purée. Drain off the excess water and store the laverbread in the refrigerator. You may find laver bread accompanying pasta dishes, seafood pizza or being served battered with freshly foraged mushrooms as part of a traditional Welsh breakfast. In its dried state, laver can be cut up and used as a wrapping for sushi. This is a traditional Japanese dish and the laver is called 'nori'. Laver is high in protein as

Green to purple-red in colour, laver clings to the base of rocks, sea walls and other firm supports.

well as vitamins C, B1, 2 and 6, and E, and contains fluoride, manganese, copper, zinc and iodine.

Purple Laver

Salicornia europaea

Marsh samphire, glasswort

multi-branched annual • grows abundantly on salt marshes •
minute flowers • can be eaten fresh or pickled

Seaside Plants

What is it?

This fleshy, small-growing annual reaches a
height of about 30 cm (12 in), but is often
shorter than this. It sometimes grows as a single
stem, but is more often found as a thick, multi-
branched bush.

What to look for

This succulent, fleshy herb has a brittle, jointed
main stem. At first glance, marsh samphire
appears to be leafless – the leaves are, in fact,
scale-like tubes that look to be part of the stem
itself. These opposite-growing leaves start off
dark green, turning pinky-red in the autumn.
The flowers, which open in August, are too
tiny to easily distinguish, and what you are
more likely to see is the flower's green bract
or yellow stamen.

Where to look

The best place to look for marsh samphire is on
sandy beaches, mudflats and on salt marshes
where it can grow so densely that it looks like a
field of grass when viewed from a distance. It
must have a sunny aspect, however, but it will
grow in very alkaline and saline soils. It is found
in abundance growing throughout Europe.

When to look for it

This plant has two seasons of interest for the
forager. In early summer (around June), the
young shoots are ready for collection, while in
late summer (August–September) you can cut or
snip the whole main stem and sideshoots. Leave
about 5 cm (2 in) of stem behind to generate
new shoots.

What does it taste like?

If you come across a patch of marsh samphire
while out walking, just pick a few young stems,
give them a rinse and pop them in your mouth.
What a wonderfully crisp, fresh, delightful
flavour they have. Although slightly salty, the
closest comparable vegetable would be the
stems of young spinach leaves.

Wash the leaves to
remove sand and grit
and you can eat the
young growing tips as
a simple snack.

Forager's checklist

- ✔ Seeds ripen in September
- ✔ Best plants are those regularly washed by the tide
- ✔ Lower branches are often as long as the plant is tall
- ✔ Stems are best picked when they are about 15 cm (6 in) long
- ✔ Flowers open in groups of three

How is it used?

You can eat the young, succulent stems raw as a simple, ready salted snack food or as a flavouring added to soups, sauces and other similar dishes. Before using marsh samphire, make sure that you wash it thoroughly to remove any sand, grit, mud or pieces of old seaweed that may be stuck to it (but do not soak the stems in water for any length of time as they quickly begin to decay). You may also want to remove the woody inner core of the stems before cooking, or you can just as easily strip the flesh away with your teeth once it is cooked. Young stems require very little cooking, so add them towards the end of the preparation time. If you are cooking the larger, older stems and branches, treat them as you would asparagus and boil or steam them, in unsalted water, for about eight minutes.

Try it in

Samphire Surprise (see page 240).

Marsh Samphire

The low-tide mark is a likely place to forage for wind-pollinated marsh samphire, which can become invasive.

GARDEN VISITORS

Many of us have grown tomatoes, brassicas and a few root vegetables in the garden or enjoyed the benefits of a row of cultivated brambles or fruiting trees, but chances are that we have overlooked some other culinary treats. Some of the 'weeds' we so assiduously remove from the beds, borders, lawns and allotments could, in fact, be very tasty garden visitors. Some caution is required, however, since plants such as red valerian and fat hen can become invasive if not kept well under control. The other type of garden visitor often ignored as a culinary treat are the edible fungi, such as the shaggy ink cap or common morel, that appear unbidden in our lawns or wood piles.

Centranthus ruber

Red valerian

hardy, drought-resistant perennial • may become invasive • showy
masses of flowers • can be cooked as greens or eaten raw

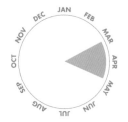

Garden Visitors

What is it?
This upright herbaceous perennial reaches
45–100 cm (18–36 in) and has a spread of
30–60 cm (12–24 in).

What to look for
The glaucous (blue-green), fragrant leaves of red
valerian grow in opposite pairs, about 5–7 cm
(2–3 in) long, and grow on stems coming from
a woody base. The lower leaves are rather
slender in shape, while those higher up are
sessile (attached without an intervening stalk).
The individual flowers, usually a purplish-red,
though sometimes lavender or white, are not
large – only about 1.5 cm (¾ in) across – but
they bloom in heavy-laden branched clusters and
make quite a show between May and August.

Where to look
This freely self-seeding plant can be found
anywhere on waste ground, rocky cliffs
(especially near the sea) and in hedgerows
where it is sunny and the soil is well drained.
However, it is just as likely to turn up in your
garden, having self-seeded itself into your
cultivated beds or taken hold on the tops of
walls or in any crevices or cracks in buildings
that are deep enough to hold the smallest

amount of soil and moisture. Red valerian is
found throughout central and southern Europe
and was introduced into Britain about 500
years ago. Where conditions are right, it can
become invasive.

Producing flamboyant spikes of flowers,
even in very little soil, red valerian
makes a colourful garden visitor.

When to look for it

The young leaves and shoots of red valerian make the best eating so confine your foraging to the spring months, before the flowers start to open. The root can be taken after the seed has ripened (or before if you want to limit propagation).

What does it taste like?

Although popular in some countries (see below) many people find the leaves, even when taken young, to be too bitter.

How is it used?

The bitter taste of red valerian means that you should use the leaves in moderation, adding just a few raw to salads to give the flavour a bit of an edge. In France and Italy the leaves are sometimes treated as a green vegetable, lightly boiled and served with butter. It is probably an acquired taste. You can, however, use the root as a flavouring in soups. Any medicinal properties assigned to red valerian are probably down to confusion with true valerian (*Valeriana officinalis*), which is a well-known and often used medicinal herb.

Forager's checklist

✔ Flowers have a strong, unpleasant scent of stale perspiration

✔ Flowers held on erect stems well above the foliage

✔ Seeds ripen June–September

✔ Produces dandelion-like seed heads that are dispersed by the wind

✔ Does not do well in prolonged periods of high humidity

Red Valerian

The warmth and protection of garden walls make them a popular growing site for this drought-resistant perennial.

Chamaemelum nobile

Common chamomile

perennial, aromatic herb • dried flowers make pot pourris and
herb pillows • used medicinally by the ancient Egyptians •
suitable for growing as a lawn

Garden Visitors

What is it?
Growing from a multi-branching, creeping
rhizome, this evergreen perennial herb reaches
a height of 15–30 cm (6–12in) and has a
spread of about twice its height.

What to look for
The stems of this low-growing plant trail along
the ground, while the feathery, fern-like leaves
are alternate and finely dissected. They are
spirally arranged and oblong in profile. The
flowers, which open between June and August
as solitary terminal heads, have a bright yellow

This drought-tolerant herb can stand up
to foot traffic and makes an aromatic
substitute for grass in garden lawns.

central disk and radiating silver-white petals,
giving them a daisy-like appearance. Flower
heads are 2–3 cm (about 1 in) across.

Can be mistaken for
Similar-looking plants are corn or field
chamomile (*Anthemis arvensis*) and mayweed
(*Anthemis cotula*). The immediate difference you
will notice is that neither of these plants has any
scent, while common chamomile smells strongly
of apples, and if further confirmation is required
the leaves of common chamomile are hairless
(glabrous) beneath while those of the mayweed
and corn chamomile are downy.

Where to look
This plant has been in cultivation a long time, so
is a likely find in old, abandoned gardens, in
empty ground bordering habitation and as a
weed growing in cultivated fields. Its creeping
habit and ability to self-seed means it could
easily become a garden visitor, finding favour
perhaps in the rockery, or taking hold in bare
patches in your lawn. Its resilience and the
aromatic qualities recommend it as a grass
substitute in lawns. Its natural range is western
Europe but it is naturalized throughout the
temperate regions of Europe.

Forager's checklist

✔ Seeds ripen August–October
✔ Daisy-like flowers
✔ Pollen may cause an allergic reaction
✔ Mat-forming plant
✔ Leaves highly aromatic when crushed

When to look for it

Common chamomile is an evergreen herb, so you can take the leaves throughout the year, though the more-important flowers, used to make tea, are available only between June and August.

What does it taste like?

The flowers are strongly, sweetly aromatic, but, rather surprisingly, have a slightly bitter flavour.

How is it used?

Although the whole of the common chamomile plant can be used as a flavouring for herbal beers, the flower heads are most prized in the kitchen. For the best flavour, collect the heads when the petals are just beginning to look a little sad and droopy. Dry them in a dry shady place in the open air. The dried flowers are used for herbal tea, though you can use fresh flowers if you prefer. Use about a teaspoon of fresh or dried flowers per cup, and leave them to infuse in boiling water for four minutes. Strain before serving. Once dried, you can store the heads for a few weeks in an air-tight container.

Chamomile has been used in folk medicine for centuries to help ease digestive problems and as a sedative.

Chenopodium album

Fat hen

widely distributed annual herb • nutritious but potentially invasive
• can be used raw or cooked • long flowering period

What is it?
An upright annual of small to medium height, reaching 30–100 cm (12–36 in), and with a spread of about 15–40 cm (6–16 in).

What to look for
The first leaves of this upright, branching annual are roughly diamond-shaped and toothed towards the tip, while the later leaves are narrow and untoothed. All leaves are mid-green, simple and opposite growing. From June to October tiny, unstalked, green flowers open in terminal clusters and in the axils of the upper leaves.

Where to look
Fat hen has a particular liking for disturbed ground, so don't be surprised to find it establishing itself in a newly laid-out garden, for example, or even growing up through cracks in your front path or back terrace. You are also likely to come across fat hen on waste ground and old muck and compost heaps. This plant has the ability to concentrate nitrates in its leaves, however, so don't take it from ground that has been fertilized (see Caution below). Fat hen probably originated in Europe, but has now been naturalized around the world.

The diamond shape and serrated edges inform us that this is a young, first leaf of the nutritious fat hen.

Forager's checklist

✔ **Must have an open, sunny position**

✔ **Inconspicuous flowers followed by fruits containing tiny black seeds**

✔ **Leaves feel clammy and have a whitish coating on the under surface**

✔ **For long-term storage, leaves can be dried or frozen**

✔ **Seeds are easier to collect once the heads have dried naturally in late autumn or early winter**

When to look for it

If you come across fat hen early in the season, late spring to early summer, you can take the whole plant for the kitchen, though you can continue collecting the leaves until the first frosts arrive. The leaves do not turn bitter as the season progresses, as so commonly happens with other plants, but they do become smaller and smaller. The season for collecting the flower heads is June–October, and the seeds ripen August–October.

What does it taste like?

Given that another of this plant's common names is wild spinach, it won't surprise you to learn that it does taste a lot like its cultivated cousin, though milder and some say with a hint of pea-pods. Fat hen is often rated as having a superior flavour to spinach.

How is it used?

The spring plants can be used whole, cut up as part of your salad ingredients – though it is not recommended to eat the raw leaves in any great quantity (see Caution below). For cooking purposes, treat the leaves, stems and shoots as you would spinach. The seed, though small and fiddly, is excellent as a food flavouring in breads, either ground down and added to the flour or sprinkled on top before baking. Soak the seed in water overnight before using. The seed also sprouts readily and then makes a fine salad addition, as do the the flower clusters, or try them in a stir-fry.

Try it in

Spicy Fat Hen and Tomatoes (see page 244).

Caution

In common with many members of its genus, fat hen contains toxic substances called saponins, though usually in quantities too small to be harmful. Most saponins pass through the body without being absorbed, and they are further broken down by cooking. However, if you suffer from rheumatism, arthritis or kidney stones you should limit your intake. Another feature of fat hen is its ability to concentrate nitrates (as does spinach). For this reason, do not use plants that have grown on land treated with fertilizers containing nitrate.

These plants, often found in cultivated garden beds, need to be strictly controlled to prevent them taking over.

Coprinus comatus

Shaggy ink cap

long fruiting season • found growing in groups • tall-growing,
scaly fungus • common garden visitor

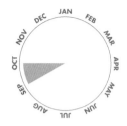

Garden Visitors

What is it?
A tall-growing fungus that, when young, looks
like an off-white egg growing straight out of the
ground, without a stem. Scales start to appear
and a stem becomes apparent as the fungus
matures. Reaches a height of 7–25 cm (3–10 in)

What to look for
You may find this tall fungus in groups, lines,
circles or dense clusters. The columnar to bell-
shaped cap is 5–15 cm (2–6 in) high and 2.5–5
cm (1–2 in) across. The cap is white with a
brown central disk, but its distinguishing feature
is the off-white to light brown scales covering the
surface. The hollow stem is smooth and white,
about 1 cm (½ in) thick, and the flesh is soft and
white throughout. Its common name of shaggy
ink cap comes from the fact that when its spores
are released the gills begin to degenerate from
the base into a black ink-like liquid.

Where to look
This fungus is commonly found on disturbed
ground, rubbish piles, roadside verges, playing
fields and, of course, garden lawns. You will
sometimes find it under trees, but it usually
prefers a more open site. Shaggy ink cap is
found throughout Europe.

When to look for it
Shaggy ink cap has a very long, productive
fruiting season. The peak months are early
autumn, around September and, especially,
October, but you are likely to find it growing
any time from April to December.

What does it taste like?
This is a mild fungus, in both taste and aroma,
and once cooked some say that it is quite
similar to an oyster mushroom.

With immature specimens, the stem
of the shaggy ink cap is almost
completely obscured by the cap.

Forager's checklist

✔ Scales on cap overlap
✔ Stems often taper towards the top and separate easily from the cap
✔ Gills are very congested
✔ Once gills have dissolved, all that remains is a flat, ragged cap on a long stem
✔ Grows best in deep, organic-rich soil

How is it used?

Fortunately, this fungus is not prone to insect infestation, but before cooking discard the stem and then wipe the cap with a damp cloth to remove any soil or detritus. The best specimens are the young caps that have not yet started to break down into black fluid. But this process starts very soon after picking, so waste no time getting them into the pot. The easiest way to cook shaggy ink caps is to slice them in half and fry them quickly in butter. Or you can coat them in breadcrumbs for deep-frying. Don't waste the older caps if you happen to have some – fry them gently on a low heat and then run them through a liquidizer and add to soup ingredients. Be warned, however, the colour of the ink may put off some diners.

Try it in

Shaggy Ink Cap Soup (see page 245).

Shaggy Ink Cap

It is not unusual to find a congregation of shaggy ink caps appearing suddenly among the grass of your lawn.

Morchella esculenta

Common morel

popular edible fungus • grows in the same place season after
season • deeply honeycombed cap • associates with deciduous trees

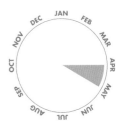

What is it?
Growing 2.5–10 cm (1–4 in) tall and with an
irregular, often non-symmetrical shaped, deeply
pitted cap 2.5–6 cm (1–2½ in) wide, this fungus
is, unfortunately, becoming an increasingly rare
fungus. It tends to grow on the same site year
after year, and those who know of a reliable
source tend to keep the location to themselves.

What to look for
The most striking feature of the common morel
is its honeycombed, pitted cap. Within the
recesses the surface varies from grey to light
brown, and this tends to darken as the fungus
matures. The sturdy stem, about 2.5 cm (1 in)
across, is hollow and forms a single chamber
with the cap, which is also hollow. The stem is
usually smooth towards the top, but grooved
near ground level. The flesh is thin and brittle.

Can be mistaken for
There are very similar-looking fungus species,
such as *Morchella rotunda* and *M. vulgaris*,
which also make good eating, but you must
be careful not to confuse these fungi with the
false morel (*Gyromitra esculenta*), which can
be fatally poisonous. The highly convoluted
cap of false morel is large, a rich brown

colour and both the hollow stem and cap have
multiple chambers, while the stem and cap of
the true morel form a single chamber. If in any
doubt, take a longitudinal slice through the
fungus and check for the chamber.

Where to look
This fungus is found throughout Europe and is
often associated with deciduous trees, especially
ash and elm. It prefers a light, well-drained
sandy or chalky soil. Other likely places to find
common morel are in woodland clearings,
established hedgerows and orchards and, if

The common morel makes excellent
eating in the spring time, which is
when it is found.

Forager's checklist

✔ **Grows abundantly after fire has cleared the land**

✔ **Apple orchards can be worthwhile hunting grounds**

✔ **On the cap, lighter-coloured rims surround the cavities**

✔ **Sweet and pleasant smell**

✔ **Cap and stem are fused together**

Look for the common morel in the undisturbed nooks and crannies of your garden, especially after spring rain.

you are fortunate, in any quiet areas at the back or edges of your garden.

When to look for it
This is an early fungus, likely to be found only in the late spring months (April and May). The best time to look is shortly after a warm downpour of rain when the soil smells rich and earthy between your fingers.

What does it taste like?
The taste and smell of the common morel is sweet and mild according to some, while others describe it as earthy, meaty or slightly peppery. Yet others say that it is simply not distinctive. Overall, this species is regarded as one of the finest.

How is it used?
Trim the bottom off the stem and check inside to see if the chamber has been colonized by

insects. The cavities in the cap are also excellent hiding places for insects and must be thoroughly washed before cooking – some people briefly blanch the fungi in boiling water. Then if you cut the morel in half lengthways you have two cut-outs for stuffing and baking. To dry morels, clean them as already described, cut them in half lengthways and thread them on cotton suspended over a radiator or in an airing cupboard until they turn crisp. Store them in a sealed jar (away from sunlight). Soak the pieces in milk to plump them up again or grind them down into powder to enhance the flavour of stews and soups.

Try it in
Morels with Wild Rice (see page 246).

HEDGEROW PLANTS

Originally planted with a wide range of tough, no-nonsense shrubs, creepers and small trees to act as field boundaries and to help control drifting snow in winter, the hedgerows that survived being grubbed up act as food-rich lifelines for a great many of our native animal species. And these wild green corridors are there for our benefit too, providing a seasonal feast of fruits and berries to enliven our often jaded taste buds.

Alliaria petiolata

Hedge garlic

unbranched biennial herb • leaves can be taken very early in the year • widely distributed • needs shady, moist conditions

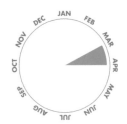

What is it?
An unbranched or minimally branched, upright biennial (sometimes annual) herb that reaches 70–100 cm (28–36 in) with a spread of about 50 cm (20 in).

What to look for
The leaves of hedge garlic are triangular to cordate (heart-shaped), mid-green and have coarsely serrated margins. In their first year, plants produce rosettes of leaves that remain low to the ground. These stay throughout the winter, becoming a mature plant in the following year. Stem leaves are alternate and about 15 cm (6 in) long (including the stem) and 2.5–6 cm (1–2½ in) across at their widest. Between April and June, small, button-like, brilliant-white, four-petalled flowers are produced in small, terminal clusters. Some plants may have a second flush in mid-summer. Seeds ripen from June to August.

Where to look
This plant does best in damp, shady locations, in open woodland, shady garden borders where the soil is kept moist to wet, in areas adjacent to drainage ditches where the ground is boggy and, of course, in hedgerows. Hedge garlic is

The dappled shade of an established hedgerow makes an ideal site for this biennial herb.

probably a European native but it has now been naturalized in many countries of the world.

When to look for it

Following a mild winter you may find hedge garlic leaves as early as February, though it is best to wait until late March to take the upper leaves and young shoots. This is when the plant is carrying flower buds but is not showing any colour. Occasionally, a new crop of leaves is produced in the autumn (September and perhaps October), but these usually don't have the depth of flavour of the spring leaves.

What does it taste like?

The smell and taste of the leaves – especially the spring leaves – is subtly of garlic with hints of mustard. The flowers and seed pods also taste of garlic, but are milder still.

How is it used?

Used raw, the young leaves and shoots impart a fresh, garlicky and mustard aroma and tang to salads, though without any of the up close and personal problems of the real stuff. Cut them up fine and blend them with blander salad leaves. They are also believed to help fortify the digestive system. The flowers and young seed pods also give a mild garlic flavour used raw. In some regions, hedge garlic is mixed with mint sauce and served with spring lamb and mutton, while in other places it is traditionally used to flavour fish, particularly herring.

Forager's checklist

✔ Rosette leaves are dark green, kidney-shaped and have scalloped edges

✔ Leaves smell strongly of garlic when crushed

✔ Flower petals are in the shape of a cross

✔ Seed, in slender pods 2.5–7 cm (1–3 in) long, is shiny black when fully ripe

Hedge garlic is self-fertile and insect-pollinated and can establish substantial clumps in shady, moist conditions.

Hedge Garlic

Humulus lupulus

Hop

vigorous, twining perennial climber • used to flavour beer for more than 1,000 years • produces male and female flowers • widely distributed

Hedgerow Plants

What is it?
This tall perennial climbing plant grows at a fast to medium rate, reaching 4–6 m (13–20 ft). It sends up new growth in the spring and then dies back to a hardy rhizome beneath the ground in autumn.

What to look for
The leaves are opposite with a stem (petiole) up to 12 cm (5 in) long. The leaves are broad and 12–15 cm (5–6 in) long. They have a heart-shaped base with between three and five lobes and the margins are coarsely serrated. The flowers are either male or female, but you will not find both sexes growing on the same plant. Flowers are yellow-green to cream-tan and the male flowers are small and open in panicles (branched clusters); the female flowers open in rounded, cone-like clusters. Flowering time is between July and August.

Where to look
This is a native British plant, as well as being native in other temperate European regions. Hop prefers the sunny margins of wooded areas, neglected waste-land areas, where there are old walls or poles for it to colonize and long runs of hedgerows where it can send its tendrils out searching for new territory. Hops are not particular about soil type (light or heavy) and it will tolerate dappled shade as well as full sun. It is drought-tolerant.

When to look for it
The best time to look for the shoots and leaves if you want to use them as a vegetable is early spring, whereas if it is the flowers you want for beer-making (you need the female flowers) then the traditional time for hop picking is the autumn month of September.

What does it taste like?
The taste of the hop leaves and shoots is said to both smell and taste 'refreshingly aromatic'.

Young hop leaves are delicious in salads. For best results, take leaves only up to mid-spring.

Forager's checklist

✔ Stems twist in a clockwise direction

✔ Flowers are fragrant

✔ Plant requires well-drained ground

✔ Seeds ripen in September and October

✔ Stems covered with stiff hairs help the vine to cling on

As well as their use in beer-making, hops have been employed as a soothing, calming tonic by traditional herbalists.

How is it used?

The young spring trimmings are delicious chopped up and fried slowly in butter. Either treat this as a vegetable in its own right or run it through a liquidizer briefly, leaving the mixture a little chunky, and add it to soups or sauces. These early shoots are also tasty raw, chopped up and mixed in with your other salad leaves. An Italian-style omelette calls for a handful of hop shoots to be fried in olive oil and added to four eggs, seasoned to taste. Cook the omelette normally until it is cooked right through.

Try it in

Hop Shoots with Eggs (see page 247).

Caution

Although not a common occurrence (about 1 in 3,000 people require treatment), handling hops can cause a skin reaction known colloquially as hop dermatitis. The pollen, too, can trigger an allergic reaction.

Prunus spinosa

Sloe, blackthorn

abundant in hedgerows • bright, white springtime bloom •
succulent berries • summer fruit • flavours gins and liqueurs •
tart flavour

Hedgerow Plants

What is it?
Juice-packed berries on a dense shrub growing
up to 6 m (20 ft) high.

Best eaten after the first frosts, the sloe is
best known as a flavouring for gin, but it
also makes great jelly and conserves.

What to look for
Look for a thick, tall bush with sharp spines
on dark, almost black, branches. Its leaves are
small – no more than 2.5 cm (1 in) – and light
green in summer, turning more yellow with time.
The flowers are small and white and appear
before the leaves in spring (March to April). The
fruit of the sloe are small, round, very dark-blue
berries that look like miniature plums; they are
covered with a pale bloom when young. Each
fruit grows singly, rather than in bunches, and
is rarely more than 1 cm (½ in) in diameter.

Where to look
The sloe is abundant in both hedgerows and
wooded areas, but it prefers full sunlight to
shady conditions. It is common throughout the
temperate regions of northern Europe. In some
countries it is cultivated for use as hedging or
as cover for game birds.

When to look for it
The fruit follow the flowers, so it is best to
look out for them from mid-April. A warm, mild
spring season may encourage earlier growth,
so if you have noticed sloe blossom then return
about four or five weeks later and the bush
should be ready for harvesting.

What does it taste like?

Biting into a sloe berry for the first time is an amazing experience. The skin bursts letting loose a soft, juicy pulp that is very tart. Most recipes include sugar to combat this fruit's acidity. At the centre of the berry is a small, hard, inedible pip.

How is it used?

The sloe has been eaten since Neolithic times and, despite its eye-watering sharpness, it is an extremely versatile fruit. It makes a delicious jelly and can be included in tarts to balance the taste of sweeter fruits, such as apple. However, it is as a base to a drink that the sloe really comes into its own. In Britain and Ireland sloe gin is popular and in the Navarra region of Spain it is made into a popular liqueur called *patxaran*.

Forager's checklist

✔ Leaves are oval and light green or yellow

✔ Branches and twigs are dark, almost black

✔ Bears dark-blue berries about 1 cm (½ in) in diameter

✔ Berries often display a misty bloom

✔ Shrub-like bush is unlikely to be in the shade

Adding to the springtime colour, the sloe flowers are an intense white and open in profusion on the bare branches.

Sloe

Ribes nigrum

Blackcurrant

typical hedgerow plant • erect, deciduous shrub • good source of
vitamin C • mid-summer fruit • can be eaten as a snack food

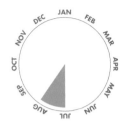

Hedgerow Plants

What is it?
This deciduous fruiting shrub reaches 1.5 m
(5 ft), sometimes even 1.8 m (6 ft) and has a
spread approximately equal to its height.

What to look for
The leaves are simple and alternate, between
5–10 cm (2–4 in) long and palmately divided
into five lobes. The leaf margins are serrated.
Drooping stalks of non-showy greenish-yellow or
reddish-green flowers, about 5 mm (¼ in) across,
open between April and May, in racemes up to
10 cm (4 in) long. The showy, edible berries

Small clusters of berries follow the
flowers, ripening to a purple-black
colour from about mid-summer.

that follow the flowers are glossy and purple-
black in colour.

Can be mistaken for
When the plant is not carrying fruit, it can be
mistaken for the redcurrant (*Ribes rubrum*) – see
pages 192–3.

Where to look
This typical hedgerow plant can be cultivated in
garden beds or grow wild in damp woodland
habitats, near drainage ditches or by streams. It
will grow in an open, sunny position, but it does
best with some dappled shade to give protection
from the afternoon sun. Blackcurrant is found
throughout temperate Europe.

When to look for it
If you are interested in the leaves of the
blackcurrant, the best time for foraging is
April–June. Most people, however, associate this
plant with its delicious berry crop, and this is
available for picking from July into August,
depending on local conditions.

What does it taste like?
Bursting with juice and managing to taste sweet
while maintaining an edge of sharpness –

Forager's checklist

✔ Leaves and stems have an odour that is musty and cat-like

✔ Soil conditions must be moist

✔ Does best where summers are cool

✔ The glossy near-black berries are about 1 cm (½ in) across

✔ Check bushes regularly as ripe blackcurrants are popular with birds

Blackcurrant

blackcurrants remain moreish while never becoming sickly. The berry contains several seeds.

How is it used?

You can eat blackcurrants raw as a healthy, vitamin-C-packed snack food, but make sure the berries are fully ripe and so at maximum sweetness. The berries are, however, more usually cooked and used as a flavouring or filling for jams, jellies and pies, ice cream and cordial. Another use of the berries is in alcoholic drinks – just leave them to steep in a brandy, gin or vodka bottle. You can use the leaves as a soup ingredient or dry them as a tea substitute. You can also add the dried leaves to other herbal teas to make up your own blend. The berries readily freeze for long-term storage.

Try it in

Wild Berry Compote (page 248).

Protected from direct light and heat by the typical hedgerow, the blackcurrant thrives if the soil is sufficiently damp.

Ribes rubrum

Redcurrant

small-growing deciduous shrub • non-showy flowers • berries can be eaten raw or cooked • mid-summer fruiting • bright red fruit

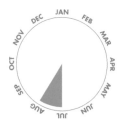

Hedgerow Plants

What is it?
A deciduous fruiting shrub reaching 1.2–1.5 m (4–5 ft), sometimes 2 m (6½ ft), and with a spread of 60–100 cm (24–36 in).

What to look for
The leaves of this usually multi-stemmed shrub are simple and alternate, 5–10 cm (2–4 in) long and palmately divided into five lobes. Leaves are arranged spirally on the stems and the margins are serrated. Drooping stalks of inconspicuous greenish-yellow flowers, about 5 mm (¼ in) across, open between April and May, in pendulous racemes 3.5–7 cm (1½–3 in) long. The showy, edible berries that follow the flowers are bright red, with 3–10 berries in each raceme.

Can be mistaken for
When the plant is not carrying fruit, it can be mistaken for the very similar-looking blackcurrant (*Ribes nigrum*) – see pages 190–1.

Where to look
This typical hedgerow plant can also be found cultivated in garden beds or growing wild in damp woodland habitats, near drainage ditches or by streams. It will grow in an open, sunny position, but it does best with some dappled shade to give protection from the afternoon sun. Redcurrant is found throughout temperate Europe.

When to look for it
For the redcurrant leaves, the best time is between April and June; for the berries, the best months are July into August, depending on local conditions.

The clusters of berries of the redcurrant hang down clear of the stems, making them easy to pick.

What does it taste like?

The redcurrant is a little more tart than its close relative, the blackcurrant. Do not eat the seeds.

How is it used?

The redcurrant does not crop as heavily as the blackcurrant, so you will have to find a sizeable patch of bushes to make a foraging trip worthwhile. A mouthful or two of berries when out walking are extremely pleasant, however, and they, like the blackcurrant, are rich in vitamin C. If you find sufficient berries for the pot, you can turn them into wonderful summer puddings, tarts, fruit soups, jams and sauces (remember to strain the cooked berries for seeds). The dried leaves make a tea (reputedly good for gout and rheumatism), but see Caution below.

Caution

The fresh leaves of the redcurrant contain small amounts of a toxic substance called hydrogen cyanide, which can, if taken in excess, lead to death.

Not usually a heavy cropper, you should find a large redcurrant patch to make a foraging trip worthwhile.

Forager's checklist

- ✔ Leaves have no odour when rubbed between your fingers
- ✔ Produces red berries up to 1 cm (½ in) across
- ✔ Likes a humus-rich, moisture-retentive soil
- ✔ Watch out for competition from birds
- ✔ On rare occasions, berries can be white or off-white

Ribes uva-crispa

Gooseberry

spiny, densely growing shrub • tolerates a range of soil conditions
• fruit usually very tart • fruiting not reliable in many regions

Hedgerow Plants

What is it?
A spiny, multi-branched shrub that makes a thicket of foliage. It reaches a height of 60–150 cm (2–5 ft) and has a spread of 1–1.8 m (3–6 ft).

What to look for
The leaves of this low-growing deciduous shrub are blunt to rounded with deeply scalloped margins, and are divided into 3–5 lobes. Gooseberry branches are protected by a formidable array of long, sharp spines, found singly or in tufts of up to three spines. The small, bell-shaped, greenish-yellow flowers – petals bent back to expose the stamens – open, either singly or in pairs, between March and May. The egg-shaped, greenish-yellow edible fruit that follows is smaller than you may be used to from cultivated bushes, but the flavour is often superior.

Where to look
If you think of hedgerows as being essentially thorny, prickly places, part of the reason for this could be the presence of gooseberry bushes, which often flourish in these uncultivated corridors. Other places to look are lightly wooded areas or woodland margins, especially if there is water nearby. Gooseberry bushes do well in the colder, northerly latitudes of Europe where they prefer a position fully open to the sun; when they grow further south, they benefit from the protection afforded by light, dappled shade.

When to look for it
Depending on local conditions, you can find gooseberry fruits ripe and ready for picking between the months of June and July through to September.

Mid-summer through to early autumn is the time to forage in hedgerows for wild-growing gooseberries.

Gooseberry

Forager's checklist

✔ Fruit is usually hairy

✔ Occasionally, purple berries are found

✔ Fruit of wild species may be a third the size of cultivated varieties

✔ Look out especially for moist soil conditions

✔ Wear gloves when picking to protect yourself from the spines.

What does it taste like?
Sweet is a relative term, and some gooseberries are described as being sweet, but really only in comparison with the ones that are extremely tart.

How is it used?
You can eat uncooked gooseberries that have been left on the bush until they are completely ripe and are at their maximum sweetness, but most people prefer to pick them earlier, when they are still very firm and very tart-tasting, for use as fillings in pies and tarts or simmered right down for making jams, chutneys and, of course, the famous gooseberry fool. You can use the young leaves in salads, but there are some concerns regarding toxicity if eaten in large quantities. See Caution, page 193.

Try it in
Gooseberry and Flapjack Tart (see page 251).

The gooseberry bush is armed with a formidable array of spines, so protect your hands when picking the fruit.

Rubus caesius

Dewberry

hairy, prickly bramble • related to the blackberry • very widely
distributed • makes a perfect snack food

Hedgerow Plants

What is it?
A sprawling, low-growing deciduous bramble
that grows to 20–40 cm (8–16 in) and with a
spread of at least 1 m (3 ft) plus.

What to look for
If you have trouble identifying the different types
of bramble before they are in fruit, the dewberry
should be a relatively easy one for you. The
distinctly three-lobed leaves are quite large and
have coarsely serrated margins, while the white
flowers, which bloom for a long time between
May and September, are large and showy, have
pronounced stamens, and petals that either fully
touch or even overlap. The berries that follow
have fewer nodules (drupes), and are produced
in less profusion, than the more usual blackberry,
and they look like they have a waxy bloom,
making them appear blue (*caesius* is Latin for
'pale blue'). Technically, 'berry' is an incorrect
term for the fruit, as each one is composed of
numerous drupelets around a central core.

Where to look
This European-wide plant prefers grassy or
bushy scrubland, heaths, the sunny edges of
woodland where it receives some dappled
shade and in the shelter and protection
provided by the hedgerow community of plants,
where it is the birds that often feast on its fruit.

When to look for it
You will find dewberry plants ready for picking
any time between July and September. The
stems are only weakly spiny, but you should
expect to receive armfuls of scratches unless
you take the precaution of wearing long sleeves
and gloves.

The dewberry flourishes among the
mixed shrubs of a typical hedgerow,
where it is often overlooked by foragers.

What does it taste like?

Be careful when picking the fruit, as it is bursting with juice and is easily damaged by rough handling. The juice is sweet and has a good depth of flavour, though there is an enjoyable edge of sharpness even when it is fully ripe.

How is it used?

The fruit is delicious whether it is eaten raw as a snack food or as part of a fresh fruit salad or cooked as a pie or tart filling, a flavouring for jellies or made into jam. Many people hold that the flavour is superior to that of blackberries. Try dipping the plump fruit, one at a time, in fresh, whipped cream lightly flavoured with a little vanilla extract. You can also use the leaves, fresh or dried, as a tea substitute.

Try it in

Dewberry and Mixed Fruit Summer Pudding (see page 250).

Dewberry

Forager's checklist

- ✔ Leaves turn red in autumn and some may stay on the stems over winter
- ✔ Requires a moist, well-drained soil
- ✔ As it ripens, fruit goes from green to red and finally to purple-blue
- ✔ Fruit is soft and tender when fully ripe, and so difficult to pick without damaging it
- ✔ Fruit seems to have a waxy finish

The flowers are showier than those of most other brambles and bloom from late spring to early autumn.

Rubus fruticosus

Blackberry

one of a great number of closely related species • a prickly,
deciduous shrub • grows quickly and can be invasive • its berries
have been eaten by man since prehistoric times

What is it?
A very prickly, untidy, deciduous bramble that quickly reaches a height of 3 m (10 ft) or more and with a spread of about the same.

What to look for
The blackberry has a scrambling habit, sending out arching, densely prickly stems that quickly root and so soon form an impenetrable thicket

Drupes turn from green to red and,
finally, when ripe in mid-summer
onwards, to a lustrous purple-black.

of growth. The savage spines are short, very sharp and curved. The leaves, which appear in March and remain until November, are lobed, prickly and have serrated margins, and change from green to shades of red in the autumn.
The flowers, which are white or pinkish-white, have five petals and many stamens. They are produced in numerous, heavy clusters between May and September. The 'berries' – technically aggregate drupes – appear after the flowers, turning purple-black as they ripen from mid-summer into autumn.

Where to look
Blackberry bushes are adaptable plants, able to thrive on poor soil and in a variety of conditions, such as grassy or bushy scrubland, heaths and wooded areas where they form a dense under-storey. The blackberry also thrives on waste land of all descriptions, railway embankments, building sites, roadside verges and in hedgerows. The blackberry is found throughout Europe and generally prefers moist soil, though it is drought-tolerant.

When to look for it
The fruits ripen between August and October. The drupes do not ripen all at once, so you can

visit the same patches time and again to collect the fruits as they become ready. In most years, September is the peak month for blackberrying. Long sleeves and gloves are recommended to protect you from the spines, unless you want to confine your picking to the easily accessible outer fruits. After the first frosts, any remaining fruits lose condition and become tasteless.

What does it taste like?
Succulent and sweet are the terms most often applied to the fruit of the blackberry. The seeds, which are too small to remove, can get between your teeth and some people regard them as a nuisance. A small price to pay.

How is it used?
This fruit is the ultimate snack food, enjoyed by the handful straight off the bush when out walking. If it is the right time of year, never go for a walk without taking a plastic bag or some other container in which to bring this wonderful fruit home. Cooked fruits are transformed into jams, pie and tart fillings, syrups and flavourings for jellies. The young leaves, once dried, make a tasty tea substitute, and you can peel the young spring shoots, picked just after they come through the ground, and use them raw as a salad ingredient. Another traditional use for blackberries is in the making of blackberry wine, often combined with elderberries.

Try it in
Blackberry and Apple Crumble (see page 249).

Forager's checklist

✔ Eating under-ripe fruits can upset your stomach

✔ Undersides of the leaves bear prickles

✔ Can be extremely variable in leaf shape due to hybridization

✔ Each drupe contains two tiny seeds

✔ New stems grow from the crowns each year

✔ Sends out tenacious creeping underground roots

Blackberry

The blackberry is a common hedgerow plant and tolerates a wide range of soil and lighting conditions.

Raspberry

erect, deciduous shrub • stems lightly armed with spines • widely distributed • luscious, usually red, fruits in late summer

Hedgerow Plants

What is it?
This perennial bush has arching, woody stems and reaches up to 2 m (6½ ft) and has a spread of about 1.5 m (5ft).

What to look for
This strongly growing perennial is normally only sparsely prickly and has peeling bark that

Small, star-shaped, off-white flowers appear from the leaf axils during the summer months.

ranges in colour from yellow to a warm brown. Leaves are palmate, alternate and divided into 3–5 leaflets, 7–12 cm (3–5 in) long. Leaves are green on their upper surface, while the underside is often silvery-white. Leaf margins are sharply serrated. Small, off-white or whitish-green nodding flowers open in clusters from the upper leaf axils between June and August, and these are followed by fruit in late summer or early autumn.

Where to look
The best places to look for raspberries are on neglected land, such as field margins, old demolition sites, railway embankments and around drainage ditches. Look on the edges of damp wooded areas or in forest clearings, on heathland and obviously, in hedgerows. It can grow in full sun or dappled shade, but needs moist soil to bring its fruit to full ripeness. This is a widely distributed plant and can be found throughout temperate Europe.

When to look
Raspberry bushes are in fruit between July and September, and the peak month for the fruit is September, though as with all these attractive and tasty fruiting species, the longer you put off

collecting, the more competition you will face from birds and other wildlife. Although raspberries are not as heavily protected with spines as blackberries, it is still a good idea to wear gloves and long sleeves.

What does it taste like?
The leaves are described as having an astringent flavour, while the berries, if fully ripe, are sweet and juicy. The fruit when picked – unlike that of blackberries that stays together – tends to separate into individual drupes, leaving a fleshy core behind.

How is it used?
Raspberries make an ideal snack food eaten straight off the bush. But bring the excess fruit home and you can make it into pies and tarts, jams and other preserves, as well as jellies and flavourings for sauces and ice creams. In addition, you can also transform the fruit into raspberry wine and raspberry vinegar. The young, tender spring shoots can be peeled and eaten raw as salad ingredients or lightly boiled or steamed and served with melted butter, as you would asparagus. The dried leaves make a popular tea substitute, or combine the leaves with other herbal teas to concoct your own blends.

Try it in
Berry Brûlée (see page 252).

Forager's checklist

✔ Fruiting stems (canes) are biennial – producing fruit on second-year wood
✔ Canes often form dense tangles of growth
✔ Leaves are prickly
✔ Old canes become scaly
✔ Raspberry fruits are slightly woolly or hairy

Raspberry

The flowers are followed by clusters of fruit, turning rich red as they ripen in late summer through to autumn.

Sambucus nigra

Elder

large shrub or small tree • flowers have a powerful aroma • cork-like bark • prolific amounts of berries produced from late summer

What is it?

A fast-growing deciduous large shrub or small tree, the elder reaches 3–10 m (10–33 ft).

What to look for

The dark-green leaves of the elder are alternate and divided into 5–7 narrow leaflets, 2.5–9 cm (1–3½ in) long, with finely serrated margins. The bark is a lighter shade of brown towards the base, becoming greyer and whiter higher up. The texture is stippled and looks a little cork-like. Crowded umbels of small, creamy-white flowers with yellow anthers first appear in June and bloom through to July. From a distance, the flowers smell pleasantly musky; close up, however, they are a little fishy. The berries that follow turn from green to red-brown and, when fully ripe, to shiny purple-black.

Where to look

The elder is a widely distributed plant, likely to be found as a component part of hedgerows, growing up on waste ground, roadside verges, scrub and heathland and in wooded areas. It does particularly well in disturbed, nitrogen-rich, moist soil, either in light, dappled shade or full sun. The elder is commonly found throughout Europe.

When to look for it

The two parts of interest are the flowers and the fruits. For the flowers, the picking season is June and July, though take only what you need and leave the rest undisturbed to become berries. For the berries, the time to look is late summer to early autumn (August–September).

The berries turn from green to red-brown before turning purple-black when they are ready for picking.

Forager's checklist

✔ **Crushed foliage has a strong, unpleasant odour**

✔ **Stands up well to atmospheric pollution**

✔ **Fruit is about 8 mm (⅓ in) in diameter**

✔ **Flower heads can be occupied by insects**

✔ **Often found growing near water**

fry them in oil until golden-brown. They are delicious served with sugar and fresh mint. Once dried, the flowers make a sweet tea (and are reputedly beneficial to women in labour).

Try it in
Elderflower and Gooseberry Jelly (see page 253).

Caution
Both the leaves and stems of the elder are poisonous. If there is any toxic substance present in the fruit, then it is at a very low concentration and it is completely destroyed by cooking.

What does it taste like?
The bitter flavour of the raw berries is not to many people's liking. The flowers, however, make a pleasant, sweet-tasting snack when eaten raw, and when cooked as a food flavouring they bring sweet, aromatic hints of muscatel.

How is it used?
Elderberries, fresh or dried, are traditionally turned into jams, jellies, preserves, chutneys, sauces, pies, tarts and, of course, elderberry wine. The dried fruits are said to be less bitter than the fresh. There is no known toxicity issue with the flowers (see Caution below) and you can eat them raw as a snack or add them as a flavouring to stewed fruits, jellies and jams. Another way to enjoy the flower heads is to dip them in a flour, egg and water batter and deep-

The creamy white blooms first appear in June. The flowers are small, but they open in crowded, nearly flat umbels.

RECIPES

Although you are likely to be familiar with at least some of the plants that have featured in the previous chapters of this book, and, indeed, you may well have used many of them in the kitchen at various times, the following chapter will hopefully provide you with a range of new recipe ideas combining familiar and less well-known ingredients.

Wild Garlic Pasta

Serves 4
Prep time 15 mins
Cooking time 30–40 mins

100 ml (3½ fl oz) olive oil, plus extra for pasta

300 g (10 oz) pasta

375 g (12 oz) onions, finely sliced

4 wild garlic cloves, crushed

500 g (1 lb) red and yellow peppers, cored, deseeded and quartered

500 g (1 lb) ripe tomatoes or 400 g (13 oz) can chopped tomatoes

salt and pepper

1 Bring at least 1.8 litres (3 pints) lightly salted water to the boil in a large saucepan. Add a dash of oil and cook the pasta for 8–10 minutes or until just tender. Drain and keep warm.

2 Meanwhile, heat the oil in a heavy-based pan and gently fry the onions and wild garlic until they are lightly coloured. Add the peppers, cover and cook over gentle heat for 10–12 minutes.

3 Add the tomatoes and season generously with salt and pepper. Cook, uncovered, until the peppers are tender and the liquid has reduced to a thick sauce. Check the seasoning and serve over the pasta.

Chocolate **Chestnut** Truffles

Makes about 24 truffles
Prep time 20 mins, plus
  cooling
Cooking time 10 mins

**250 g (8 oz) plain dark chocolate,
  chopped**

125 g (4 oz) puréed chestnuts

50 ml (2 fl oz) brandy

1 teaspoon vanilla extract

125 ml (4 fl oz) double cream

**cocoa powder, finely chopped Brazil
  nuts or finely grated chocolate, for
  dusting**

1 Put the chocolate in a heatproof bowl and set it above a saucepan filled with hot water. Make sure the bowl does not touch the water. Leave until the chocolate has melted, stirring once or twice.

2 Put the chestnut purée in a bowl and mix in the melted chocolate and remaining ingredients. Leave the mixture to cool until it is set enough to roll into balls.

3 Roll the mixture into walnut-sized balls and dust them with the cocoa powder, nuts or chocolate. The truffles will keep in the refrigerator for up to a week.

Walnut and Two-cheese Pasta

Recipes

Serves 4
Prep time 10 mins
Cooking time 15 mins

4 tablespoons olive oil, plus extra for pasta

300 g (10 oz) pasta

2 garlic cloves, chopped

125 g (4 oz) walnut pieces

2 plum tomatoes, cut into wedges

50 g (2 oz) Camembert cheese, cut into pieces

50 g (2 oz) Gruyère cheese, grated

bunch of chives, snipped

salt

1 Bring at least 1.8 litres (3 pints) lightly salted water to the boil in a large saucepan. Add a dash of oil and cook the pasta for 8–10 minutes or until just tender. Drain and keep warm.

2 Meanwhile, heat the oil in a nonstick pan and cook the garlic, walnuts and tomatoes for 1 minute, stirring.

3 Add the drained pasta to the walnut sauce and toss well. Reduce the heat.

4 Add both cheeses to the sauce, followed by all except 2 tablespoons of the snipped chives. Toss well with the pasta, spoon on to warm plates and serve garnished with the reserved snipped chives.

Olive and Orange Salad

Serves 4
Prep time 10–15 mins
Cooking time 5 mins

2 teaspoons cumin seeds

4 large oranges

125 g (4 oz) olives, pitted and halved

50 ml (2 fl oz) olive oil

1 tablespoon harissa paste (optional)

1 crisp lettuce, torn into bite-sized pieces

salt

sprigs of dill, to garnish

1 Heat a small, heavy-based pan, add the cumin seeds and dry-fry until fragrant. Transfer to a grinder and grind to a powder.

2 Remove the rind from one of the oranges with a zester and set aside.

3 Peel the oranges with a sharp knife, carefully removing all the pith. Working over a bowl to catch the juice, cut out the segments from the oranges and discard the pips.

4 Put the oranges and olives in a bowl with the juice. Whisk together the oil, harissa paste (if used) and roasted cumin seeds. Season with salt to taste, then pour the dressing over the olives and oranges and toss together.

5 Arrange the lettuce leaves on a serving dish. Add the orange and olive salad, garnish with the reserved orange rind and sprigs of dill and serve.

Recipes

Arame **Almond** Risotto

Serves 4
Prep time 10 mins
Cooking time 30 mins

1.5 litres (2½ pints) vegetable stock

pinch of saffron threads

2 bay leaves

25 g (1 oz) dried porcini mushrooms, chopped

2 dessertspoons dried arame seaweed, crushed

3 teaspoons bouillon powder

1 tablespoon avocado oil

2 tablespoons coconut oil

1 small onion, finely chopped

2 garlic cloves, finely chopped

375 g (12 oz) arborio rice

500 ml (17 fl oz) dry white wine

50 g (2 oz) toasted pine nuts

125 g (4 oz) frozen peas

4 tablespoons ground almonds

1 tablespoon chopped basil

salt and pepper

hemp oil, to serve

1 Pour the vegetable stock into a large pan, bring to the boil, then reduce the heat to a simmer. Add the saffron, bay leaves, mushrooms, arame and 1 teaspoon bouillon powder, stir and leave to simmer.

2 Heat the avocado oil and 1 tablespoon coconut oil in a large, nonstick frying pan, add the onion and garlic and fry gently until translucent. Pour the rice into the pan, stir to coat the grains and fry for about 5 minutes. Do not let the rice brown.

3 When the rice is hot add a ladleful of stock and stir for 2–3 minutes. When the rice has absorbed the liquid, add further ladlefuls of stock, stirring until each is absorbed.

4 Add the wine, a glass at a time, and continue stirring and cooking over a low heat.

5 When the rice has cooked, stir in the remaining coconut oil together with the pine nuts, peas, salt and pepper.

6 Remove the bay leaves, pour in any remaining stock, together with the arame and mushrooms. Remove the rice from the heat, stir thoroughly, cover and leave to stand for 5 minutes.

7 Gently warm the ground almonds and mix with the remaining bouillon powder. Stir the basil into the risotto, then transfer to a warm serving dish. Sprinkle with ground almonds, pepper and a drizzle of hemp oil.

Cherry Clafoutis

Serves 4
Prep time 15 mins
Cooking time about 30 mins

500 g (1 lb) ripe cherries

15 g (½ oz) butter

icing sugar, to dust

Batter

75 g (3 oz) plain flour

25 g (1 oz) caster sugar

3 eggs

225 ml (7½ fl oz) milk

few drops vanilla extract

1 Pit the cherries over a bowl to avoid wasting any juice.

2 Make the batter by whisking together all the ingredients.

3 Grease a 1.5–1.8 litre (2½–3 pint) soufflé dish with the butter and heat for a few minutes. Add the cherries and any juice to the dish, then pour over the batter.

4 Bake in a preheated oven, 200°C (400°F), Gas Mark 6, for 30 minutes or until the batter is well risen. Dust with icing sugar and serve at once.

Recipes

Cep Pancakes

Serves 4
Prep time 15 mins, plus
  standing
Cooking time 40 mins

**50 g (2 oz) mozzarella cheese,
chopped**

sunflower oil, for frying

salt and pepper

sprigs of chervil, to garnish

Pancakes

125 g (4 oz) spinach

125 g (4 oz) plain flour

300 ml (½ pint) skimmed milk

1 egg

ground nutmeg

Filling

25 g (1 oz) cep mushrooms

1 tablespoon olive oil

1 onion, chopped

1 garlic clove, chopped

**250 g (8 oz) button mushrooms,
quartered**

1 tablespoon wholemeal plain flour

2 tablespoons single cream

1 Make the pancakes. Cook the spinach briefly and press it to extract excess water. Put it in a food processor with the flour, milk and egg, season with salt and pepper and add nutmeg to taste. Blend until smooth, then pour into a jug and leave to stand for 30 minutes.

2 Meanwhile, make the filling. Cover the ceps with boiling water and leave to soak for 15 minutes. Drain and chop the mushrooms, reserving the liquid.

3 Heat the oil in a nonstick frying pan and fry the onion until softened, add the garlic, button mushrooms and ceps and cook for 2 minutes, stirring occasionally. Stir in the flour, then add 125 ml (4 oz) of the reserved mushroom liquid or water and stir until thickened. Stir in the cream and season to taste.

4 Heat a little oil in a 15 cm (6 in) nonstick frying pan and pour a little batter into the pan. Cook until golden underneath, then turn over and cook the other side. Repeat until all the batter is used up. Stack the cooked pancakes on a warm plate.

5 Put a tablespoon of the mushroom mixture on each pancake, roll up and place in a greased, shallow ovenproof dish. Sprinkle with the mozzarella and bake in a preheated oven, 190°C (375°F), Gas Mark 5, for 15 minutes until heated through. Serve immediately, garnished with chervil sprigs.

Lime and Mixed Leaf Salad with Strawberries

Serves 4–6
Prep time 10 mins

**250 g (8 oz) mixed salad leaves
(e.g. lime, nasturtium, dandelion,
rocket, escarole, red oakleaf,
salad burnet, frisé, radicchio,
lamb's lettuce)**

**handful of fresh herb sprigs, with
flowers (e.g. fennel, chives,
dill, mint)**

**250 g (8 oz) small strawberries,
hulled**

salt and pepper

Dressing

150 ml (¼ pint) natural yogurt

1 tablespoon lemon juice

1 teaspoon clear honey

½ teaspoon Dijon mustard

salt and pepper

1 Tear the leaves into large pieces and put in a salad bowl or on individual plates. Scatter over the herbs.

2 Halve the strawberries, or leave them whole if very small. Add to the salad with a little salt and pepper.

3 Make the dressing by beating the ingredients together in a small bowl until smooth. Season with salt and pepper to taste.

4 Pour the dressing over the salad and toss lightly. Serve immediately.

Bilberry Pie

Recipes

Serves 6–8
Prep time 25–30 mins, plus
    chilling
Cooking time about 45 mins

Pastry

250 g (8 oz) plain flour

1 teaspoon salt

175 g (6 oz) unsalted butter, diced

4–5 tablespoons iced water

Filling

500 g (1 lb) bilberries

200 g (7 oz) sugar

25 g (1 oz) plain flour

1 teaspoon grated orange rind

¼ teaspoon grated nutmeg

2 tablespoons orange juice

1 teaspoon lemon juice

1 Make the pastry. Sift the flour and salt into a bowl. Rub in the butter until the mixture resembles breadcrumbs, then mix with enough water to make a pliable dough. Form into a ball, wrap in clingfilm and chill for at least 20 minutes.

2 Divide the dough in 2. Roll out 1 piece on a lightly floured surface and use it to line a 20–23 cm (8–9 in) pie dish or flan tin.

3 Make the filling. Put the bilberries in a bowl and sprinkle over the sugar, flour, orange rind and nutmeg. Toss until evenly mixed, then add the orange and lemon juices and toss again. Spoon the mixture into the lined pie dish and spread out evenly.

4 Roll out the remaining dough on a lightly floured surface for the lid. Seal the edges well and make several slits in the top. Bake in a preheated oven, 180°C (350°F), Gas Mark 4, for about 45 minutes or until the pastry is golden-brown. Serve warm or cold.

Fettuccine with **Chanterelles**

Serves 4
Prep time 15 mins
Cooking time 30 mins

300 g (10 oz) chanterelles, morels or other wild mushrooms

500 ml (17 fl oz) chicken stock

15 g (½ oz) butter

1 tablespoon olive oil, plus extra for pasta

bunch of spring onions, finely chopped

4 tablespoons dry white wine

300 g (10 oz) fresh fettuccine verde

350 ml (12 fl oz) whipping cream or crème fraîche

2 tablespoons toasted pine nuts

salt and pepper

1 Thinly slice the mushrooms, reserving any discarded pieces of stem or skin.

2 Pour the stock into a saucepan and bring to the boil. Add the mushroom peelings and cook over a medium-high heat until reduced to 125 ml (4 fl oz). Strain through a sieve and discard the peelings.

3 Melt the butter with the oil in a large, nonstick frying pan. Add the mushrooms and spring onions and cook, stirring, until the mushrooms begin to render liquid. Add the wine and cook over high heat until the liquid has nearly evaporated.

4 Meanwhile, bring at least 1.8 litres (3 pints) lightly salted water to the boil in a large saucepan. Add a dash of oil and cook the pasta for 4–8 minutes or until just tender. Drain and keep warm.

5 Add the reduced stock and cream to the mushroom mixture. Bring to the boil and reduce the sauce to half its original volume. Season to taste with salt and pepper. Add the drained pasta and pine nuts to the pan and toss to coat with the sauce. Serve immediately.

Chicken of the Woods Ragout

Serves 6
Prep time 25 mins
Cooking time 1 hour

3 tablespoons olive oil

1 large red onion, diced

500 ml (17 fl oz) vegetable stock

250 ml (8 fl oz) carrot juice

2 swedes, peeled and finely diced

500 g (1 lb) squash, peeled and finely diced

1 butternut squash, about 500 g (1 lb), peeled and finely diced

500 g (1 lb) chicken of the woods, wiped clean and stemmed

175 g (6 oz) pitted prunes, coarsely chopped

½ teaspoon dried thyme

½ teaspoon dried marjoram

salt and pepper to taste

2 tablespoons finely chopped parsley, to garnish

1 Heat the oil in a large, heavy-based saucepan over medium heat. Add the onion and cook for about 5 minutes or until soft.

2 Add the stock and carrot juice, increase the heat to high and bring to the boil. Add the swedes and squashes, reduce the heat to medium-low and simmer, uncovered, for 30 minutes.

3 Add the mushrooms, prunes and herbs and cook for a further 15–20 minutes or until all the vegetables are tender. Season to taste with salt and pepper. Ladle into warm bowls and serve garnished with parsley.

Bolete Pie

Serves 6
Prep time 20 mins
Cooking time 40–45 mins

250 g (8 oz) can tomatoes

375 g (12 oz) bolete fungi

125 g (4 oz) shelled walnuts

1 carrot, finely chopped

1 red onion, chopped

1 red pepper, deseeded and
  chopped

1 tablespoon chopped dates

1 teaspoon mustard powder

500 (1 lb) puff pastry (thawed if
  frozen)

1 tablespoon cornflour

1 teaspoon carob powder

2 tablespoons rapeseed oil

1 dessertspoon yeast extract

1 tablespoon balsamic vinegar

1 tablespoon chopped parsley

1 teaspoon pepper

1 dessertspoon sesame seeds, to
  garnish

1 Blend the tomatoes to a purée, transfer to a large, heavy-based saucepan and bring to the boil. Reduce the heat to a simmer and add the mushrooms, walnuts, carrot, onion, red pepper, dates and mustard powder. Stir well and simmer, covered, for 15 minutes.

2 Meanwhile, divide the pastry in 2. Roll out 1 piece to 5 mm (¼ in) thick and use it to line a greased 30 cm (12 in) pie dish. Bake blind in a preheated oven, 180°C (350°F), Gas Mark 4, for 7 minutes.

3 Combine the remaining ingredients in a jug and gradually pour into the stew, stirring constantly as it thickens.

4 Spoon the stew into the pie crust. Roll out the remaining pastry and cover the pie, sealing the edges with a little water.

5 Sprinkle the pastry with sesame seeds and bake for 25–30 minutes or until puffed and golden.

Winter Cress Salad

Serves 6 as a first course
Prep time 20 mins
Cooking time 15 mins

**125 g (4 oz) winter cress, stalks
removed**

**2 yellow peppers, skinned, cored
and deseeded**

12 round slices white country bread

2 garlic cloves, halved and scored

2–3 tablespoons olive oil

3 large tomatoes, peeled and halved

1 tablespoon chopped basil

6 round slices goats' cheese

**8 yellow and red cherry tomatoes,
halved**

pepper

Dressing

1–2 tablespoons lemon juice

½ tablespoon white wine vinegar

6 tablespoons olive oil

1 Wash and dry the winter cress and pile it loosely on a serving dish.

2 Cut the flesh of the yellow peppers into long strips and set aside.

3 Toast the bread under the grill, then rub the slices on both sides with the cut garlic cloves. Drizzle a little olive oil over them.

4 Squeeze the tomatoes to express the seeds and juice. Lay a tomato half on each slice of bread and sprinkle with chopped basil. While the bread is still hot, lay a slice of goats' cheese on each slice.

5 Make the dressing by mixing together all the ingredients. Pour half over the winter cress and toss.

6 Lay the tomato- and cheese-topped bread over and around the edges of the dish, interspersed with the halved cherry tomatoes and strips of yellow pepper. Grind pepper over the whole dish and drizzle the rest of the dressing on top.

Wild Strawberry Ice Cream

Serves 8
Prep time 20 mins, plus
    freezing

375 g (12 oz) wild strawberries

15 g (½ oz gelatine)

450 ml (¾ pint) evaporated milk, chilled

175 g (6 oz) caster sugar

2 tablespoons lemon juice

8 wild strawberries, to decorate

1 Blend the strawberries in a food processor and sieve to remove the pips. This should give around 300 ml (½ pint) purée.

2 Soak the gelatine in 3 tablespoons water in a small bowl and stand it over a pan of simmering water. Stir until dissolved and add to the strawberry purée.

3 Whisk the evaporated milk until thick, then add the sugar, strawberry purée and lemon juice. Turn into a freezer-proof container. Cover, seal and freeze for 1 hour.

4 Remove from the freezer and stir well, then re-freeze until solid. Transfer to the refrigerator 1 hour before serving to soften. Serve decorated with the wild strawberries.

Parsley and Herb Salad

Serves 4
Prep time 10 mins, plus
    soaking

50 g (2 oz) bulgar wheat, washed

2 bunches of spring onions, chopped

**2 tomatoes, skinned, deseeded and
    chopped**

**50 g (2 oz) parsley, leaves only,
    chopped**

4 tablespoons chopped mint

3 tablespoons olive oil

3 tablespoons lemon juice

salt and pepper

**inner leaves of 1 cos lettuce, to
    garnish**

1 Soak the bulgar wheat in a bowl of cold water for 30 minutes, then drain it and squeeze dry. Put it in a clean bowl and mix gently with the spring onions.

2 Add the tomatoes and herbs, season with salt and pepper and mix well. Stir in the olive oil and lemon juice. Pile into a shallow bowl and serve garnished with lettuce leaves.

Watercress Soup

Serves 6
Prep time 15 mins
Cooking time 40 mins

200 g (7 oz) watercress

40 g (1½ oz) butter

1 tablespoon olive oil

1 potato, peeled and diced

900 ml (1½ pints) hot chicken stock

150 ml (¼ pint) double cream

salt and pepper

1 Reserve 6 sprigs of watercress and chop the rest roughly.

2 Heat the butter and oil in a large, heavy-based saucepan and gently cook the chopped watercress for 5 minutes. Add the potato and cook for another 5 minutes, stirring often.

3 Add the stock, bring to the boil and season to taste with salt and pepper. Simmer for 25 minutes, then remove from the heat and leave to cool slightly.

4 Blend the soup, adding the cream, then reheat gently in a clean pan. Serve in warm bowls with a sprig of watercress in each one.

Recipes

Comfrey Fritters

Recipes

Serves 4
Prep time 15 mins
Cooking time 12 mins

comfrey leaves

vegetable oil, for frying

lemon quarters, to garnish

Batter

125 g (4 oz) plain flour

pinch of salt

2 tablespoons sunflower oil

150 ml (¼ pint) soda water or sparkling water

1 egg white

1 Trim the stalks from the comfrey, rinse the leaves carefully under cold running water, then shake and pat them dry on kitchen paper.

2 Shortly before serving, heat a large pan of vegetable oil to 180°C (350°F), or until it is hot enough to brown a small cube of bread in 20 seconds.

3 Meanwhile, make the batter. Sift the flour with the salt into a food processor. With the motor running, add the oil, then gradually add the soda or sparkling water, beating constantly and stopping when the batter has reached the consistency of thick cream. Whisk the egg white until stiff and fold it into the batter.

4 Dip each leaf in the batter, shaking off the excess, then drop it into the hot oil. Cook a few leaves at a time for about 3 minutes, then lift them out and drain on kitchen paper while you cook the next batch. As soon as the leaves have drained, transfer to a warm dish. Serve immediately, garnished with lemon quarters.

Coriander and Black Bean Soup

Serves 4–6
Prep time 15 mins, plus
   cooling
Cooking time 1¾ hours

**500 g (1 lb) dried black beans,
soaked overnight**

3 tablespoons olive oil

1 large red onion, finely chopped

3 large garlic cloves, finely chopped

**3 red chillies, deseeded and finely
chopped**

2 tablespoons tomato purée

**600 ml (1 pint) hot chicken or
vegetable stock**

pinch of cayenne pepper

1½ tablespoons lime juice

salt and pepper

To garnish

**150 ml (¼ pint) crème fraîche or
soured cream**

3–4 tablespoons chopped coriander

1 Drain the beans and cover them with fresh cold water. Bring to the boil and cook for 10 minutes, then reduce the heat and simmer for 50 minutes or until the beans are soft. Leave to cool for 1 hour, drain the beans in a colander standing over a large bowl. Reserve about 500 g (1 lb) of the cooked beans and purée the rest in a food processor with 600 ml (1 pint) of the cooking liquid. Reserve the rest of the bean stock.

2 Heat the oil in a large, heavy-based saucepan and fry the chopped onion for 5–6 minutes. Add the garlic and chillies and cook, stirring frequently, for another 2–3 minutes. Add the tomato purée and cook, stirring, for a further 4–5 minutes. Add the stock, bring to the boil and simmer for 30 minutes.

3 Stir in the puréed beans, the reserved whole beans, the cayenne and season with salt and pepper to taste. If the soup is too thick, add a little of the reserved cooking liquid. Stir in the lime juice. If possible, allow to stand for the flavours to develop for a few hours and reheat before serving.

4 Spoon the soup into warm bowls and serve with a dollop of crème fraîche or soured cream and a sprinkling of coriander.

Wild Mushroom Ring Mould

Serves 3–4
Prep time 15 mins
Cooking time 1 hour

50 g (2 oz) wild rice

50 g (2 oz) basmati rice, rinsed

50 g (2 oz) roasted buckwheat

Filling

4 tablespoons olive oil

4 shallots, chopped

2 garlic cloves, finely chopped

375 g (12 oz) mixed wild mushrooms, cut in large pieces

125 g (4 oz) coarsely chopped parsley

salt and pepper

Sauce

150 ml (¼ pint) soured cream

150 ml (¼ pint) natural yogurt

1 Cook the wild rice in 750 ml (1¼ pints) lightly salted, boiling water for 40–45 minutes. Cook the basmati rice in 750 ml (1¼ pints) lightly salted, boiling water for 10 minutes. Cook the buckwheat in 175 ml (6 fl oz) lightly salted, boiling water, covered, for about 14 minutes or until all the water has been absorbed. Mix the grains together thoroughly and pack into an oiled ring mould holding about 1.2 litres (2 pints). Cover loosely with foil and keep warm in a low oven.

2 Heat the oil in a nonstick frying pan and cook the shallots for 2 minutes. Add the garlic and cook for 1 minute more, then add the mushrooms. Cook gently, tossing frequently, for about 8 minutes or until the mushrooms have softened. Stir in the parsley and season to taste with salt and pepper.

3 Make the sauce by mixing together the soured cream and yogurt, beating until smooth.

4 Turn out the mould on to a flat dish and spoon some of the mushrooms into the centre. Serve the rest in a separate bowl and the sauce (at room temperature) in another bowl.

Tansy Pudding

Serves 4
Prep time 15 mins, plus
   standing
Cooking time 45–50 mins

50 g (2 oz) soft white breadcrumbs

300 ml (½ pint) single cream

4 eggs, beaten

150 ml (¼ pint) spinach juice

2 tablespoons chopped tansy leaves

2 tablespoons sugar

½ teaspoon ground nutmeg

1 Put the breadcrumbs in a bowl. Bring the cream to the boil, then pour it over the breadcrumbs and leave, covered, to stand for 15 minutes.

2 Stir in the eggs, spinach juice, tansy, sugar and nutmeg. Turn the mixture into a buttered dish and bake in a preheated oven, 160°C (325°F), Gas Mark 3, for 45–50 minutes or until the pudding is firm.

Recipes

Pear, **Chicory** and Gorgonzola Bruschetta

Recipes

Makes 8
Prep time 15 mins
Cooking time 15 mins

2 chicory heads

50 g (2 oz) butter

2 large, ripe pears, cored and sliced

4 slices of crusty Italian bread, preferably 1 day old

1 garlic clove, peeled but left whole

2 tablespoons walnut oil

175 g (6 oz) Gorgonzola cheese, diced

1 Remove and discard the outer leaves from the chicory. Cut each chicory head lengthways into four slices.

2 Melt half the butter in a large, nonstick frying pan and fry the pear slices for 2–3 minutes until lightly browned on both sides. Remove with a slotted spoon and set aside.

3 Add the remaining butter to the pan and fry the chicory slices for 5 minutes on each side until softened and golden.

4 Meanwhile, cut each slice of bread in half and grill under a preheated grill for 1 minute on each side. Rub each side with the garlic clove and then drizzle liberally with walnut oil.

5 Top each bruschetta with the cooked chicory and pear slices, scatter the diced cheese over the pears and return to the grill for 1–2 minutes until bubbling and golden. Serve immediately.

Braised Chinese **Puffballs**

Serves 4
Prep time 15 mins
Cooking time 15 mins

250 g (8 oz) firm bean curd

4 tablespoons vegetable oil

2–3 tablespoons finely sliced puffballs

125 g (4 oz) carrots, peeled and sliced

125 g (4 oz) mangetout, trimmed

125 g (4 oz) Chinese leaves, sliced

125 g (4 oz) sliced bamboo shoots or whole baby sweetcorn

1 teaspoon sugar

1 tablespoon light soy sauce

1 teaspoon cornflour

1 tablespoon water

1 teaspoon sesame seed oil, to finish (optional)

salt

1 Cut each cake of bean curd into about 12 small pieces. Put them in a saucepan of lightly salted, boiling water for 2–3 minutes or until they are firm. Remove with a perforated spoon and drain.

2 Heat about half the oil in a heavy-based saucepan, add the pieces of bean curd and fry until lightly browned on both sides. Remove the bean curd.

3 Add the remaining oil to the pan, then add the vegetables and stir-fry for about 1–2 minutes. Return the bean curd to the pan, add 1 teaspoon salt, the sugar and soy sauce and stir well. Cover, reduce the heat and braise for 2–3 minutes.

4 Mix the cornflour to a smooth paste with the water. Pour the paste over the vegetables and stir. Increase the heat to high to thicken the sauce, then sprinkle in the sesame seed oil. Stir briefly and serve immediately.

Hot **Vetch** and Chicken Salad

Serves 4 as a first course or
2 as a main course
Prep time 10 mins
Cooking time 10–13 mins

3 tablespoons olive oil

2 chicken breasts, cut into strips

**125 g (4 oz) peeled butternut
squash, diced**

125 g (4 oz) cooked, peeled vetch

1 teaspoon crushed, dried chillies

1 cos lettuce

handful of rocket

small bunch of flat leaf parsley

1 courgette, grated

salt and pepper

1 Heat the oil in a large pan and add the chicken and diced butternut squash. Cook for 8–10 minutes or until the chicken starts to brown and the squash is soft but still holds its shape.

2 Slice the vetch in half and add them to the pan along with the chillies. Cook for a further 2–3 minutes or until the vetch are heated through. Season with salt and pepper and set aside in a warm place.

3 Tear the lettuce leaves into pieces and put them in a large serving bowl. Add the rocket and parsley leaves, along with the grated courgette, and toss to mix. Just before serving, add the hot chicken and squash mixture and serve immediately.

Parasol Platters

Serves 2
Prep time 5 mins
Cooking time 20–25 mins

2 large parasol mushrooms

2 tablespoons olive oil, plus extra for greasing

2 spring onions, chopped

½ red pepper, deseeded and chopped

1 small courgette, chopped

4 olives, pitted and chopped

2 tablespoons porridge oats

1 tablespoon chopped basil

1 tablespoon soy sauce

1 tablespoon lime juice

salt and pepper

mixed salad leaves, to serve

1 Wipe the mushrooms with damp kitchen paper, then remove the stalks and chop them.

2 Heat the oil in a nonstick frying pan and gently fry the chopped mushroom stalks, spring onions, red pepper, courgette, olives and oats until the oats are golden. Stir in the basil, soy sauce and lime juice.

3 Lightly oil the mushroom caps and place them, gill side up, on a baking sheet. Spoon the oat mixture on to the mushrooms, season with salt and pepper and bake in a preheated oven, 180°C (350°F), Gas Mark 4, for 15–20 minutes or until the caps start to soften.

4 Serve the hot mushrooms immediately on a bed of mixed salad leaves.

Blewit Baskets

Serves 2
Prep time 15 mins
Cooking time 15 mins

4 tablespoons avocado oil

1 red onion, chopped

375 g (12 oz) blewit mushrooms,
  stalks finely chopped

50 g (2 oz) pine nuts

2 garlic cloves, finely chopped

25 ml (1 fl oz) brandy

50 ml (2 fl oz) vegetable stock

1 tablespoon soy sauce

8 sheets filo pastry, each 30 cm
  (12 in) square

75 ml (3 fl oz) soya cream, plus
  extra for drizzling

1 tablespoon sweet chilli sauce, plus
  extra for drizzling

1 tablespoon maple syrup

1 lime, sliced, to garnish

1 Heat 2 tablespoons oil in a heavy-based saucepan and fry the onion, mushrooms, pine nuts and garlic until golden-brown. Stir in the brandy, stock and soy sauce, then remove from the heat and set aside.

2 Take 1 sheet of filo pastry and lightly brush the surface with some of the remaining oil. Place another sheet on top and brush with oil. Cut the double thickness in half, place one half in a diamond shape over the square below to make an 8-pointed star.

3 Drape the prepared pastry over a small, foil-wrapped baking potato. Brush the pastry with oil and place on a baking sheet. Repeat with the remaining filo sheets until you have the basis of 4 filo baskets. Cook in a preheated oven, 180°C (350°F), Gas Mark 4, for about 10 minutes or until crisp and brown.

4 Stir the soya cream into the mushrooms, followed by the chilli sauce and maple syrup. Return to a simmer.

5 Carefully lift the baskets from their supports and fill with the mushroom mixture. Add drizzles of soya cream and chilli sauce to each basket and serve garnished with a slice of lime.

Marjoram Fish Soup

Serves 6
Prep time 20 mins
Cooking time 1¼ hours

1½ tablespoons olive oil

25 g (1 oz) butter

1 small onion, chopped

1 leek, chopped

1 carrot, chopped

1 celery stick, chopped

1 garlic clove, chopped

2 tomatoes, chopped

1 small bay leaf, crumbled

½ tablespoon dried *herbes de
  Provence*

1–1.25 kg (2–2½ lb) mixed white
  fish, cut into bite-sized pieces

4 tablespoons vodka

1 litre (1¾ pints) very hot water

pinch of saffron

1 tablespoon chopped marjoram

1 tablespoon chopped thyme

½ teaspoon crushed red peppercorns

salt and pepper

6 slices French bread, dried in the
  oven, to garnish

1 Heat the oil and butter in a heavy-based saucepan and cook the vegetables for 3 minutes or until they are brown. Add the garlic and tomatoes, then the bay leaf and herbs. Season to taste with salt and pepper and cook for a further 3 minutes. Add the fish, stirring well to mix the pieces with the vegetables and herbs. Pour over the vodka and continue to cook gently, stirring, for another 2–3 minutes. Add the hot water and bring slowly to the boil. Cover the pan and simmer for 1 hour.

2 Towards the end of the cooking time, tip the saffron into a small bowl and add a couple of spoonfuls of the hot stock. Leave to infuse. When the soup is cooked leave it to cool for a while, then pick out any big, bony pieces of fish and discard them. Flake and reserve some of the best pieces of fish (discarding skin and bones) and push the rest of the soup through a coarse sieve, mashing the fish and vegetables against the sides.

3 Transfer the soup to a clean pan and reheat gently, adding the saffron infusion and more salt and pepper if needed. Stir in the reserved fish, marjoram, thyme and peppercorns.

4 Spoon into warm bowls and garnish each with a slice of bread.

Bistort and Chickpea Sabzi

Serves 4
Prep time 5 mins
Cooking time 20 mins

1 tablespoon vegetable oil

1 teaspoon cumin seeds

½ teaspoon coarsely ground
   coriander seeds

1 small onion, finely chopped

250 g (8 oz) fresh bistort

200 g (7 oz) can chopped tomatoes

1 teaspoon chilli powder

1 tablespoon dhana jeera (spice
   mixture)

1 teaspoon amchur (dried mango
   powder)

1 teaspoon soft brown sugar

1 tablespoon fresh lime juice

400 g (13 oz) can chickpeas,
   drained and rinsed

175 ml (6 fl oz) water

salt and pepper

1 Heat the oil in a large, nonstick frying pan and add the cumin and coriander seeds and the onion. Stir-fry until the onion is soft and light brown, then add the bistort and tomatoes and stir well.

2 Add the chilli powder, dhana jeera, amchur, sugar and lime juice and stir. Cook for 1–2 minutes, then add the chickpeas and water. Season with salt and pepper, cover and simmer gently, stirring occasionally, for 10 minutes. Serve hot.

Wild Plum and Almond Filo Pie

Serves 6
Prep time 15 mins
Cooking time 35–40 mins

1 kg (2 lb) wild plums, halved and stoned

2 tablespoons lemon juice

50 g (2 oz) blanched almonds, chopped

50 g (2 oz) caster sugar

250 g (8 oz) filo pastry (thawed if frozen)

50 g (2 oz) butter, melted

icing sugar, for dusting

1 Mix together the plums, lemon juice, almonds and caster sugar in a bowl.

2 Place 1 sheet of filo pastry over a greased 20 cm (8 in) flan tin. Brush with butter and place a second sheet on top of the first but at an angle. Continue layering and buttering the filo, with each successive sheet at an angle to the previous ones, until only 2 sheets remain. Gently press down the filo sheets so that they take the shape of the tin, with the excess pastry overlapping the edge.

3 Fill the pastry case with the plum mixture, then layer the remaining 2 sheets of filo on top, brushing each with butter. Scrunch the overlapping edges of the pastry all round the top edge of the pie.

4 Brush the pie with any remaining butter and bake in a preheated oven, 190°C (375°F), Gas Mark 5, for 35–40 minutes or until the pastry is crisp and golden-brown. Dust with icing sugar and serve warm or cold.

Sorrel Salad

Recipes

Serves 4
Prep time 15 mins

2 small lettuces

10 sorrel leaves, cut into strips

10 sprigs of chervil

**5 marigolds, petals only, or 10
  nasturtiums**

Dressing

1 tablespoon lemon juice

1 tablespoon white wine vinegar

4 tablespoons olive oil

pinch of sugar

pinch of mustard powder

salt and pepper

1 Separate the lettuces into leaves, wash them and drain well. Pile them into a bowl and lay the sorrel and chervil on top.

2 Make the dressing by mixing together all the ingredients. Pour it over the salad, then toss well. Scatter the marigold petals or the whole nasturtiums on top and serve.

Dandelion Delight

Serves 3–4 as a first course
Prep time 15 mins
Cooking time 5–6 mins

**125–175 g (4–6 oz) dandelion
leaves**

**4 thin rashers of streaky bacon, rind
removed, cut into strips**

pepper

Croûtons (optional)

2 tablespoons sunflower oil

**2 slices dry white bread, crusts
removed**

**1 large garlic clove, halved and
scored**

Dressing

3 tablespoons sunflower oil

1 tablespoon white wine vinegar

1 Rinse the dandelion leaves under running water, pat them dry on kitchen paper and pile loosely in a bowl.

2 Fry the bacon gently until crisp and drain on kitchen paper.

3 Make the croûtons (if used). Heat the oil and fry the bread. Drain on kitchen paper and rub each side with the cut garlic clove. Cut each slice into small squares.

4 Make the dressing by mixing together the oil and vinegar. Scatter the croûtons over the leaves with the bacon. Sprinkle with pepper and pour over the dressing. Toss to mix well and serve as soon as possible, while the bacon and croûtons are still warm.

Thyme Risotto

Recipes

Serves 3–4
Prep time 15 mins
Cooking time 20–25 mins

3 tablespoons olive oil

2 shallots, finely chopped

1 garlic clove, finely chopped

250 g (8 oz) arborio rice, washed
and drained

750 ml (1¼ pints) hot chicken stock

1½ tablespoons chopped robust
herbs, such as thyme, lovage and
oregano

pinch of saffron

1½ tablespoons chopped tender
herbs, such as dill, chervil,
tarragon

40 g (1½ oz) Parmesan cheese,
grated

1 Heat the oil in a heavy-based pan and cook the shallots for 3 minutes.
Add the garlic and cook for another minute.

2 Add the rice to the pan, stir it in the oil for about 1 minute to coat the
grains, then add half the stock and the robust herbs. Put the saffron in a
small bowl, pour over 2–3 tablespoons of the remaining hot stock and
set aside.

3 Simmer the rice in the stock, stirring, for about 8 minutes or until
the stock has almost all been absorbed. Add the saffron and half
the remaining stock. When that has been absorbed, the rice will
probably be tender. If not, add the remaining stock and cook for a
few minutes longer.

4 Just before serving, stir in the tender herbs, transfer to a serving dish
and sprinkle over the grated Parmesan. Serve immediately.

Grilled **Asparagus**

Serves 1
Prep time 5 mins
Cooking time 10 mins

25 g (1 oz) butter, plus extra to drizzle

1–2 tablespoons olive oil, plus extra to drizzle

6–8 fresh asparagus spears, trimmed

salt and pepper

¼ lemon, to garnish

1 Melt the butter with the oil in a small saucepan over a low heat. Lay the prepared spears on a preheated hot grill pan or barbecue, and brush with the oil and butter mixture. Reduce the heat slightly to allow the asparagus to cook through without burning and cook for about 5 minutes without turning.

2 Turn the asparagus, brush again with the oil and butter and cook for a further 5 minutes until the asparagus is tender, well seared and slightly wilted.

3 Remove the asparagus from the grill with tongs and transfer to a warm plate. Season with salt and pepper and garnish with slices of lemon. Drizzle over a little olive oil or melted butter and serve immediately.

Borage Tart

Serves 4
Prep time 20 mins, plus
    chilling
Cooking time 40 mins

Pastry

175 g (6 oz) plain flour, sifted

½ teaspoon caster sugar

75 g (3 oz) unsalted butter, diced

2–3 tablespoons iced water

Filling

300 ml (½ pint) single cream

3 borage flowers

3 egg yolks

50 g (2 oz) caster sugar

1 egg white, stiffly beaten

1 Make the pastry. Place the sifted flour in a bowl with the sugar, add the butter and rub in with your fingertips until the mixture resembles fine breadcrumbs. Add enough iced water to make a firm dough. Wrap it in clingfilm and chill in the refrigerator for about 30 minutes.

2 Turn out the dough on to a lightly floured surface, roll it out and line a 20 cm (8 in) flan tin. Prick all over with a fork, line with crumpled foil weighed down with beans and bake in a preheated oven, 190°C (375°F), Gas Mark 5, for 15–20 minutes.

3 Meanwhile, make the filling. Put the cream and borage in a small saucepan and heat gently. When hot, but not yet boiling, remove from the heat and stand, covered, for 10 minutes. Beat the egg yolks with the sugar, reheat the cream and pour through a strainer on to the eggs, beating well. Fold in the egg white and then pour the mixture into the pastry case. Bake for 20 minutes, until risen and golden-brown. Serve immediately.

Good King Henry's Nuts

Serves 4
Prep time 15 mins
Cooking time 10–12 mins

5 tablespoons olive oil

50 g (2 oz) pine nuts or flaked almonds

1 large onion, finely chopped

2 garlic cloves, crushed

1 kg (2 lb) small Good King Henry leaves

juice of 1 orange and grated rind of ½ orange

freshly grated nutmeg

salt and pepper

1 Heat 2 tablespoons oil in a large, nonstick frying pan. Add the pine nuts or almonds and fry, stirring frequently, until lightly browned. Use a slotted spoon to transfer the nuts to kitchen paper to drain.

2 Add half the onion and garlic to the pan and fry until beginning to soften. Add half the Good King Henry and cook over a high heat for 4–5 minutes until the leaves have wilted and most of the liquid has evaporated. Transfer the leaf mixture to a warm colander.

3 Heat 2 tablespoons oil in the pan and cook the remaining onion, garlic and Good King Henry. Transfer the first batch of leaves from the colander to a warm serving dish before adding the second batch to the colander.

4 Meanwhile, whisk together 1 tablespoon olive oil and the orange juice and rind. Season with grated nutmeg and salt and pepper.

5 Add the remaining leaves to the serving dish and mix with the dressing. Scatter with the nuts and serve.

Recipes

Samphire Surprise

Serves 4
Prep time 20 mins
Cooking time 25 mins

250 g (8 oz) thin samphire spears

375 g (12 oz) new potatoes

2 kg (4 lb) crab meat

4 tablespoons olive oil, plus extra for drizzling

4 tablespoons lime juice

6 spring onions, sliced

2 tablespoons chopped fresh coriander

pinch of chilli powder

500 ml (17 fl oz) mayonnaise

salt and pepper

1 Cook the samphire spears in a large pan of unsalted, boiling water for 1 minute. Drain and refresh under cold running water, pat dry and set aside.

2 Cook the potatoes in a saucepan of lightly salted, boiling water for 10–12 minutes. Drain, refresh under cold water and set aside.

3 Place all the crab meat in a large bowl, add the oil, 2 tablespoons lime juice, the spring onions and the coriander. Season with chilli powder and pepper and toss well.

4 Mix the mayonnaise with the remaining lime juice and toss half with the cooked potatoes. Toss the samphire spears with a little extra olive oil and arrange them on the serving plates. Top with the potatoes and the crab mixture and serve with the remaining mayonnaise.

Sea Beet Cannelloni

Serves 4–6
Prep time 20 mins, plus
    cooling
Cooking time about 1 hour

**750 g (1½ lb) fresh sea beet leaves,
stalks removed**

50 g (2 oz) butter

**250 (8 oz) ricotta or cottage cheese,
sieved**

75 g (3 oz) Parmesan cheese, grated

pinch of grated nutmeg

2 large eggs

12 large cannelloni tubes

1 teaspoon olive oil

25 g (1 oz) flour

300 ml (½ pint) milk

4 tablespoons bran cereal

salt and pepper

1 Wash the sea beet, place it in a pan with the water that clings to the leaves and heat gently for 3–4 minutes or until wilted. Drain in a colander, pressing out all the moisture, then chop finely.

2 Melt half the butter in a pan, add the sea beet and stir well. Remove from the heat. Beat the ricotta or cottage cheese and half the Parmesan into the sea beet and season with salt, pepper and nutmeg. Beat in the eggs. Set aside to cool.

3 Cook the cannelloni tubes in plenty of salted, boiling water with the oil for about 10 minutes or until they are just tender. Drain, refresh in cold water and drain again. Dry thoroughly with kitchen paper. Set aside to cool.

4 Melt the remaining butter in a pan, stir in the flour and cook for 1 minute. Remove from the heat and gradually stir in the milk. Bring to the boil, season with salt and pepper and simmer for 5 minutes. Adjust the seasoning if necessary.

5 Use a teaspoon to spoon the filling into the cannelloni tubes and place them in a greased, shallow baking dish. Pour the sauce over and sprinkle with the remaining Parmesan mixed with the bran cereal. Bake in a preheated oven, 180°C (350°F), Gas Mark 4, for 35–40 minutes or until the topping is brown and crusty.

Recipes

Finocchio **Fennel**

Serves 4
Prep time 15 mins
Cooking time 30 mins

625 g (1¼ lb) fennel bulbs

1 thick lemon slice

1 tablespoon vegetable oil

25 g (1 oz) butter

25 g (1 oz) grated Parmesan cheese

salt and pepper

fennel fronds, to garnish

1 Trim the fennel bulbs and remove any discoloured skin with a potato peeler. Cut vertically into pieces 1.5 cm (¾ in) thick. Place in a pan with a pinch of salt, the lemon and oil and add sufficient boiling water to cover. Cook for 20 minutes or until just tender. Drain well.

2 Melt the butter in a gratin dish or shallow, flameproof casserole, add the fennel and turn to coat. Season with salt and pepper and sprinkle with the grated Parmesan.

3 Place under a preheated medium grill until lightly browned. Serve immediately, garnished with fennel fronds.

Sea Kale Salad

Serves 4–6
Prep time 20 mins
Cooking time 5 mins

250 g (8 oz) green beans

375 g (12 oz) sea kale

3 slices wholemeal bread

3 tablespoons olive oil

1 cos lettuce

50 g (2 oz) pine nuts, toasted

**50 g (2 oz) Parmesan cheese,
 freshly grated**

Dressing

2 tablespoons olive oil

2 tablespoons cider vinegar

1 egg yolk

1 garlic clove, crushed

1 Cut the beans and sea kale into pieces 5 cm (2 in) long. Cook for 2 minutes in a large pan of boiling water. Drain and plunge into iced water. Drain again and wrap in a clean tea towel.

2 Remove the crusts from the bread and cut into 1 cm (½ in) squares. Heat the oil in a frying pan, add the bread and fry until the cubes are golden-brown all over. Drain on kitchen paper.

3 Wash and dry the lettuce and arrange the leaves on a large platter. Combine the beans, sea kale, croûtons, pine nuts and Parmesan and spoon on top of the lettuce.

4 Make the dressing by whisking the ingredients together. Pour over the salad and serve immediately.

Spicy **Fat Hen** and Tomatoes

Serves 4–6
Prep time 15 mins
Cooking time 20–25 mins

1 kg (2 lb) fat hen leaves

3 tablespoons vegetable oil

2 large onions, thinly sliced

2 garlic cloves, thinly sliced

150 g (5 oz) fresh root ginger, peeled and thinly sliced

2 teaspoons chilli powder

2 teaspoons turmeric

2 teaspoons garam masala

2 teaspoons coriander seeds

1 teaspoon ground coriander

1 teaspoon cumin seeds

425 g (14 oz) can tomatoes

salt and pepper

1 Wash the fat hen thoroughly and shake it dry. Remove any thick stalks and cut the leaves into strips 2.5 cm (1 in) wide.

2 Heat the oil in a large, heavy-based pan, add the onions and garlic and fry gently over a moderate heat for about 5 minutes or until they are golden and soft.

3 Add the ginger and cook gently for 5–6 minutes. Stir in the chilli powder, turmeric, garam masala, coriander seeds, ground coriander and cumin seeds. Season to taste with salt and pepper and cook for 1 minute.

4 Toss in the fat hen and mix well to coat in the spice mixture. Add the tomatoes with their juice and bring to the boil, stirring. Add enough boiling water to prevent the fat hen from sticking to the base of the pan. Simmer for 5–10 minutes or until the leaves and tomatoes are cooked and serve immediately.

Shaggy Ink Cap Soup

Serves 4–6
Prep time 20 mins
Cooking time 6–8 mins

900 ml (1½ pints) chicken stock

175 g (6 oz) shrimps

50 g (2 oz) Szechuan pickled vegetables, sliced

50 g (2 oz) can bamboo shoots, drained and shredded

4 shaggy ink caps, sliced

2 celery sticks, sliced diagonally

½ cucumber

2 tablespoons Chinese wine or sherry

2 tablespoons soy sauce

1 tablespoon red wine vinegar

25 g (1 oz) ham, diced

1 spring onion, finely chopped

1 Bring the stock to the boil in a large, heavy-based saucepan, add the shrimps, pickled vegetables, bamboo shoots, mushrooms and celery and simmer for 5 minutes.

2 Cut the cucumber into 5 cm (2 in) long matchsticks. Add them to the pan with the Chinese wine or sherry, soy sauce, vinegar and ham and cook for 1 minute.

3 Transfer to warm bowls, sprinkle over the spring onion and serve immediately.

Recipes

Morels with Wild Rice

Serves 2
Prep time 10 mins, plus
    soaking
Cooking time about 30 mins

150 g (5 oz) wild rice, well rinsed

50 g (2 oz) butter

**150 g (5 oz) fresh morels, rinsed,
    trimmed and halved lengthways**

75 ml (3 fl oz) double cream

1 tablespoon brandy

salt and pepper

1 Put the wild rice in a pan of lightly salted, boiling water and cook for 18–20 minutes until the grains begin to split. Drain well.

2 Meanwhile, melt half the butter in a heavy-based pan, add all the mushrooms and cook over a medium heat for 2–3 minutes. Season to taste with salt and pepper and add the cream and brandy. Reduce the heat and continue cooking until the liquid has almost all evaporated. Transfer the mushrooms to a bowl, cover and keep warm.

3 Melt the remaining butter in the pan, add the wild rice and reheat, stirring to coat the grains with the juices. Season to taste and serve topped with mushrooms.

Hop Shoots with Eggs

Serves 4 as a first course
Prep time 15 mins
Cooking time 15 mins

375 g (12 oz) young hop shoots

4 slices white country bread, 1 cm (½ in) thick, crusts removed

50 g (2 oz) butter, melted

2 hard-boiled eggs, shelled and roughly chopped

salt and pepper

1 Treat the hop shoots exactly like asparagus: trim them to length, wash well and tie in bundles. Bring a large pan of lightly salted water to the boil, drop in the hop shoots and cook for about 10 minutes or until tender when pierced with a skewer. Drain in a colander.

2 Meanwhile, toast the bread and put 1 piece on each of 4 plates. Arrange the hop shoots over the toast, pour the melted butter on top, scatter the chopped egg over all and sprinkle with salt and pepper. Serve immediately.

Wild Berry Compote

Serves 6
Prep time 10 mins, plus
    cooling
Cooking time 10 mins

**500 g (1 lb) mixed redcurrants,
    blackcurrants and blackberries**

125 g (4 oz) caster sugar

250 g (8 oz) raspberries

whipped cream, to serve

1 Put the currants and blackberries in a heavy-based saucepan with the sugar. Cook gently over a low heat, stirring occasionally, for 10 minutes or until tender.

2 Remove from the heat, add the raspberries and set aside to cool.

3 Spoon the fruit into individual bowls and serve with whipped cream.

Blackberry and Apple Crumble

Serves 4–6
Prep time 20 mins
Cooking time 25–30 mins

500 g (1 lb) cooking apples, peeled, cored and sliced

1 tablespoon lemon juice

50–75 g (2–3 oz) caster sugar

50 ml (2 fl oz) water

2 tablespoons marmalade

125 g (4 oz) blackberries

Topping

40 g (1½ oz) unsalted butter, diced

75 g (3 oz) plain flour

40 g (1½ oz) demerara sugar

1 Put the apples in a heavy-based saucepan with the lemon juice, caster sugar (to taste) and water and cook gently for 3–5 minutes or until the apples begin to soften. Mix in the marmalade and blackberries and transfer to a shallow, ovenproof dish.

2 Meanwhile, make the topping by rubbing the butter into the flour. Stir in the sugar to make breadcrumbs.

3 Scatter the topping over the fruit mixture, pressing it down slightly. Place in a preheated oven, 200°C (400°F), Gas Mark 6, for 20–25 minutes or until the crumble topping is golden. Serve hot or cold.

Recipes

Dewberry and Mixed Fruit Summer Pudding

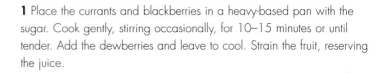

Recipes

Serves 4
Prep time 20 mins, plus
   chilling
Cooking time 10–15 mins

500 g (1 lb) mixed redcurrants, blackcurrants and blackberries

125 g (4 oz) caster sugar

250 g (8 oz) dewberries (or raspberries)

8 slices white bread, crusts removed

whipped cream, to serve

1 Place the currants and blackberries in a heavy-based pan with the sugar. Cook gently, stirring occasionally, for 10–15 minutes or until tender. Add the dewberries and leave to cool. Strain the fruit, reserving the juice.

2 Cut 3 circles of bread the same diameter as a 900 ml (1½ pint) pudding basin. Cut the remaining bread to fit round the sides of the basin. Soak all the bread in the reserved fruit juice.

3 Line the base of the basin with a bread circle, then arrange the shaped bread around the sides. Pour in half the fruit and place another circle of bread on top. Cover with the remaining fruit, then top with the remaining bread circle.

4 Cover with a saucer small enough to fit inside the basin and put a 500 g (1 lb) weight on top. Chill in the refrigerator overnight. Turn out on to a serving plate and pour over any remaining fruit juice. Serve with whipped cream.

Gooseberry and Flapjack Tart

Serves 4–6
Prep time 25 mins
Cooking time 35–40 mins

Pastry

175 g (6 oz) plain flour

1 teaspoon ground cinnamon

75 g (3 oz) chilled unsalted butter,
  diced

25 g (1 oz) desiccated coconut

1 egg yolk

Filling

500 g (1 lb) gooseberries

25 g (1 oz) caster sugar

2 tablespoons orange juice

50 g (2 oz) unsalted butter

2 tablespoons golden syrup

50 g (2 oz) light muscovado sugar

50 g (2 oz) porridge oats

25 g (1 oz) desiccated coconut

1 teaspoon ground cinnamon

1 Make the pastry. Put the flour and cinnamon in a bowl, add the butter and rub it in with your fingertips until the mixture resembles fine breadcrumbs. Add the desiccated coconut. Stir in the egg yolk and 2–3 tablespoons cold water to make a firm dough.

2 Knead the dough briefly on a lightly floured surface, then roll it out and line a 20 cm (8 in) pie plate. Fill with crumpled foil and bake in a preheated oven, 200°C (400°F), Gas Mark 6, for 15 minutes. Reduce the oven temperature to 180°C (350°F), Gas Mark 4.

3 Fill the pie case with the gooseberries and sprinkle with caster sugar and orange juice.

4 Heat the butter, syrup and muscovado sugar in a saucepan, stirring to make a smooth sauce. Remove the pan from the heat and stir in the oats, desiccated coconut and ground cinnamon.

5 Spread the oat mixture over the fruit, return the tart to the oven and bake for 20–25 minutes or until the flapjack topping has browned and the fruit is tender. Serve warm or cold.

Berry Brûlée

Recipes

Serves 4
Prep time 10 mins, plus
    chilling
Cooking time 2 mins

250 g (8 oz) blueberries

250 g (8 oz) raspberries

**350 ml (12 fl oz) Greek yogurt
or fromage frais**

**4–6 tablespoons soft dark
brown sugar**

1 Mix together the blueberries and raspberries and spoon them into
4 heatproof dishes or into a single large dish.

2 Spoon the yogurt or fromage frais over the berries and smooth
the top. Chill the puddings in the refrigerator overnight or until
you need them.

3 Sprinkle the sugar over the yogurt or fromage frais in an even layer
and place the dishes on a baking tray. Grill under a preheated hot grill
for 1–2 minutes or until the sugar has melted and is bubbling in places.
Serve immediately.

Elderflower and Gooseberry Jelly

Serves 6
Prep time 20 mins, plus
   chilling
Cooking time 15 mins

500 g (1 lb) gooseberries

450 ml (¾ pint) apple juice

4 elderflower heads, tied in muslin

75 g (3 oz) caster sugar

1 teaspoon agar agar powder

75 ml (3 fl oz) single cream

sprigs of mint, to decorate

1 Put the gooseberries into a pan with 300 ml (½ pint) apple juice and the elderflower heads. Cover and cook gently until the gooseberries are soft.

2 Remove the elderflower heads from the pan, squeezing out as much juice as possible.

3 Purée the fruit and sieve to remove the tops and tails. Add the sugar and stir until dissolved. Set aside 75 ml (3 fl oz) of the purée.

4 Put the remaining apple juice in a small pan, sprinkle over the agar agar and leave to soak for 5 minutes. Bring to the boil and simmer for 3–4 minutes until dissolved, then add to the purée. Spoon the purée into 6 decorative moulds, each holding 125 ml (4 fl oz), and chill until set.

5 Mix the cream with the reserved gooseberry purée. Turn the jellies out on to serving plates, surround each with some sauce and decorate with mint sprigs.

Recipes

Index

Index

Acknowledgements

Executive Editor Jessica Cowie
Project Editor Emma Pattison
Executive Art Editor Leigh Jones
Designer 'ome Design
Production Manager Lousie Hall
Picture Librarian Sophie Delpech

Picture Acknowledgements

Main photography © Nature Photographers Limited/Paul Sterry.

Other photography: Alamy/June Green 21 bottom right, 191. Corbis UK Ltd/Eric Crichton 193; /Frank Young 73. Frank Lane Picture Agency/Leo Batten 24, 90; /Richard Becker 113, 228; /Nigel Cattlin 11, 199; /Gary K. Smith 177, 244. Garden Picture Library/David Cavagnaro 221; /Mark Winwood 107. Leigh Jones 201, 252. Nature Photographers Ltd/Frank B. Blackburn 65, 216; /Brinsley Burbidge 9, 47, 81, 110, 147, 223, 227, 238; /Robin Bush 117, 143, 230; /Bob Chapman 173; /Andrew Cleave 103, 154, 160, 161, 167, 208; /Andrew Davies 98; /Phil Green 69; /Kate Hanford 99; /Barry Hughes 19 bottom, 116; /E. A. Janes 26, 59, 182, 189; /Owen Newman 181, 246; /David Osborn 18, 25 top right, 62, 63, 66, 70, 94, 215; /Jim Russell 180. Photolibrary Group/David Cavagnaro 93; /Michael Diggin 2, 13, 105; /Vaughan Fleming 111; /Michel Viard 6. Science Photo Library/Carl Schmidt-Luchs 72, 217.